QUICK HABITAT FIN

Hardwood Forests

Mature forest found on rolling or sloping upland terrain. High, closed canopy. Mostly red fall color. Little understory growth.

Mixed Hardwoods and Softwoods

Mature Hardwoods with scattered pines rising above the canopy, and occasional patches of other evergreen trees.

Successional Forests

Young forest found on abandoned farmlands and areas where the land has been cleared or disturbed in the distant past. Trees not tall.

Shrublands

Shrub masses found in recently abandoned fields or low, flat areas. May include scattered trees.

Farmlands

Cultivated lands or grazed areas. Fallow fields.

Reforested Lands

Plantations of evergreen trees in distinct rows. Tree canopy uniform and even-aged.

Wooded Swamps

Treed areas with saturated soils most of the year and frequently standing water.

Marshes and Wet Meadows

Saturated stands of cattails or grass-like plants. Open water areas common, especially in spring.

Beaver Flows and Creeks

Flowing water, and flooded meadows and woods behind beaver dams.

Gulfs and Bogs

Unique landscape features.

i

THE TUG HILL REGION

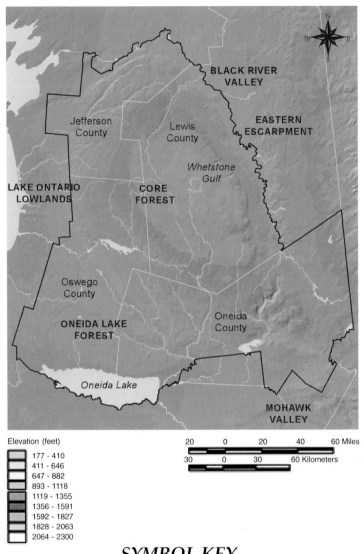

Elevation (feet)

- 177 - 410
- 411 - 646
- 647 - 882
- 893 - 1118
- 1119 - 1355
- 1356 - 1591
- 1592 - 1827
- 1828 - 2063
- 2064 - 2300

20   0   20   40   60 Miles
30   0   30   60 Kilometers

SYMBOL KEY

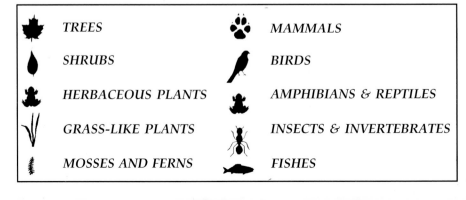

TREES		MAMMALS	
SHRUBS		BIRDS	
HERBACEOUS PLANTS		AMPHIBIANS & REPTILES	
GRASS-LIKE PLANTS		INSECTS & INVERTEBRATES	
MOSSES AND FERNS		FISHES	

TUG HILL

A FOUR SEASON GUIDE
TO THE NATURAL SIDE

TUG HILL

A FOUR SEASON GUIDE
TO THE NATURAL SIDE

Illustrated and Edited by Robert McNamara
Contributing Writers:

John Cecil	*Lee B. Chamberlaine*
Peter Gaskin	*Glenn Johnson*
Donald E. Moore III	*Lisa St. Hilaire*

North Country Books
Utica, New York

A joint publication with:

Tug Hill Tomorrow Land Trust

TUG HILL
A Four Season Guide to the Natural Side

Copyright 1999
by
Tug Hill Tomorrow Land Trust

First Edition

Printed & bound in Hong Kong, China by
Book Art Inc., Toronto

ISBN 0-925168-76-9

Library of Congress Cataloging-in-Publication Data

Tug Hill : a four season guide to the natural side / illustrated and edited by Robert
McNamara ; contributing writers, John Cecil ... [et al.].-- 1 st ed.
   p. cm.
   Includes bibliographical references (p.).
   ISBN 0-925168-76-9 (pbk.)
   1 . Natural history--New York (State)--Tug Hill Region. I. McNamara, Robert, 1951-
II. Cecil, John, 1933-

QH105.N7 T84 1999
508.747'5--dc21

                            99-050099

Published by
North Country Books, Inc.
311 Turner Street
Utica, New York 13501

DEDICATION

To the people of Tug Hill
who have worked diligently to
protect the region's quality of
life for the benefit of us all.

CONTENTS

QUICK HABITAT FINDER GUIDE .... *i*
REGIONAL MAP .... *ii*
FOREWORD.. *xi*
PREFACE... *xiii*
ACKNOWLEDGEMENTS.................…..………..... *xv*

PART ONE - INTRODUCTION

ABOUT THE GUIDE.................................. 3
TUG HILL HABITATS............................... 7
VISUAL GLOSSARY................................ 11
THE REGION...................................... 13

PART TWO - UPLANDS

HARDWOOD FORESTS
   Narrative............................……..... 19
   Illustrations 27
   Facts, Tips, and Lore 37
MIXED HARDWOODS AND SOFTWOODS
   Narrative...............…................... 51
   Illustrations 57
   Facts, Tips, and Lore 67
SUCCESSIONAL FORESTS
   Narrative...............…................... 79
   Illustrations..................................... 83
   Facts, Tips, and Lore......................... 89
SHRUBLANDS
   Narrative...............…................... 97
   Illustrations..................................... 101
   Facts, Tips, and Lore......................... 109
FARMLANDS
   Narrative...............…................... 117
   Illustrations..................................... 123
   Facts, Tips, and Lore......................... 131

REFORESTED LANDS
Narrative... 145
Illustrations................................... 147
Facts, Tips, and Lore...................... 149

PART THREE - LOWLANDS

WOODED SWAMPS
Narrative... 155
Illustrations................................... 159
Facts, Tips, and Lore...................... 163
MARSHES AND WET MEADOWS
Narrative... 169
Illustrations................................... 177
Facts, Tips, and Lore...................... 183
BEAVER FLOWS AND CREEKS
Narrative... 195
Illustrations................................... 203
Facts, Tips, and Lore...................... 213
GULFS AND BOGS (Fens)
Narrative... 223
Illustrations................................... 227
Facts, Tips, and Lore...................... 229

PART FOUR - APPENDIX

GLOSSARY................................... 235
BIBLIOGRAPHY.......................... 239
INDEX.. 241
SPECIES LISTS............................ 247
THE WRITERS............................. 259

FOREWORD

Welcome to Tug Hill Tomorrow's regional natural history guide! We hope this resource will serve to entertain, engage and inform you about our unique corner of the world. We hope that our book will inspire you to get out there and enjoy this truly wonderful area firsthand, increasing your own intimate knowledge of the plants and animals in our big backyard. We hope that it will also increase your ability to identify the impact of your own activities on this fragile environment, and prompt you to take action, however small or large, to protect and conserve the vital natural resources you encounter.

Tug Hill Tomorrow was formed in response to an expressed local need, and incorporated as a private, nonprofit land trust and education organization in 1991. The organization works to retain the region's forest, farm, recreation and wild lands by offering a variety of private land protection programs, developing and distributing regionally-focused educational materials, and conducting research. Fulfilling our mission requires strategies that address the concerns of private landowners, farmers, loggers, recreationists, individual communities, and multi-town councils. Tug Hill Tomorrow works to supplement local efforts to protect Tug Hill's unique environment and its residents' way of life.

Some individuals have looked at our weather-worn region and concluded that an influx of development is what is necessary to improve the area's economy. To be sure, a certain amount of economic development and community growth is needed to keep local economies vital. However, the larger majority of area residents and visitors seem to envision a future that protects and/or enhances the area's natural resource base as a way of maintaining what they hold most dear, and what makes Tug Hill so appealing as a home or destination. We hope that this book will educate and emphasize the high quality and abundance of Tug Hill's natural resources, and help to promote further conservation and stewardship of its very special character.

Thanks again for your interest in our publication. If you would like more information about Tug Hill Tomorrow, our programs or materials, please don't hesitate to contact us any time. Enjoy the book – and we hope to see you out on the trail!

Linda Irwin Gibbs
Executive Director

Tug Hill Tomorrow Land Trust
P O Box 6063, Watertown, NY 13601
Phone: 315-785-2382   Fax: 315-785-2574
Email: THTomorrow@imcnet.net
Web Site: http://www.imcnet.net/~thtomorr/THThomepage.html

PREFACE

DISCOVER THE NATURE OF THE HILL

There are fascinating events happening within the diverse plant communities on Tug Hill across the dramatic span of seasonal changes that you can experience if you know when and where to look. This guide is designed to accompany you into the heart of the forest and field to discover those events and to help you understand more about the plants and animals that make up the vital Tug Hill ecosystem.

The varied natural terrain and the effect of the population's use of the land over time is responsible for a tremendous diversity of species on the Hill. Recognizing the different cover types (*habitats*) is key to finding and identifying the diverse wild inhabitants. Most species have specific habitat preferences; you are not likely to find an Eastern Bluebird in the interior of a hardwood forest and you will not have much luck seeing a Scarlet Tanager in an open field. Habitat preferences are even more specific in some cases; an Ovenbird will be found scratching around in the leaves on the forest floor while a Red-eyed Vireo spends all its time in the *canopy* (the 'ceiling' over the forest formed by the intermeshed uppermost branches). Such specialization allows more species to make use of the same habitat without competing with each other. When you know where and how to look, animals and plants are easier to find and identify. Knowing the occupants of the habitats and their inter-relationships will lead to a greater understanding of the whole ecosystem. Understanding the whole ecosystem is crucial to wise use and stewardship of our precious natural resources.

This guide presents a cross section of species of flora and fauna that is a representative sample from each habitat. The general categories of subjects presented are Trees, Shrubs, Herbaceous Plants, Ferns, Mosses, Grass-like Plants, Mammals, Birds, Amphibians, Reptiles, Insects, Other Invertebrates, and Fishes. Each subject is presented in the section covering the habitat in which it is most likely found.

There are other reference books cited in the bibliography for further reading on specific topics. There are many guides that cover the species present in the region. This guide describes the specific cover types on Tug Hill and offers clues to help find and identify some of the plants and animals likely to be found in each habitat in a non-technical, easy to use format.

ACKNOWLEDGEMENTS

This publication was made possible by the generous support of...

- Black River Environmental Improvement Association (BREIA)
- The Environmental Support Center
- NYS Tug Hill Commission
- Northern New York Community Foundation
- Harden Furniture
- Cotton-Hanlon, Inc.

The Tug Hill Tomorrow Land Trust's volunteer Board of Directors, past and present:

- David Bruce, Watertown
- Bob Boice, Watertown
- John Cecil, Adams Center
- John Cheney, Redfield
- John Constable, Sr., Watertown
- Greg Gardner, Watertown
- Liz Giuliani, Redfield
- Howard Leitner, Turin
- Warren Mathis, West Leyden
- Paul Miller, Blossvale
- Doug Murray, Copenhagen
- Harold Petrie, Parish
- Larry Rudd, Mannsville
- Craig Schrader, Rodman
- Bob Sauer, Camden
- Ron Service, Constableville
- Stacey Smith, Remsen
- Hertha Thayer, Parish
- Joan Williams, Watertown
- Thomas J. Yousey, III, Chases Lake

Thanks also for their vision, commitment, and invaluable assistance

- Linda Blair Garrett, past Executive Director
- Robert Quinn, Executive Director, NYS Tug Hill Commission

PART ONE
INTRODUCTION

ABOUT THE GUIDE

TUG HILL HABITATS

The intricate pattern of various shades of green that covers the Tug Hill region in summer is categorized by 10 habitat types, each presented in a separate section. The habitat types are grouped into lowlands and uplands according to the presence or absence of standing water at various times of the year. With a little practice, you will find that these habitats are visually distinct. There may be minor variations within each habitat due to the presence of a different species of plant or two, but the general appearance will still be distinct from other habitat types. The distribution and extent of the habitats is shown on the map; *Generalized Tug Hill Habitats*. The map can be used as an indicator of the prevalent habitat for a given area though the scale is too small to try to pinpoint a specific habitat on a particular piece of property.

SPECIES SCOPE

The focus of this *Guide* is to present a wide cross section of the plants and animals inhabiting Tug Hill. It is not intended to cover any species type in exhaustive detail, but to offer a sampling of many different species types shown in association with each other. These groups of interrelated species form the distinct habitats that are covered in the *Guide*. The species selected are not necessarily the most common but are the ones that can be easily found by the casual naturalist. Hence, species such as the robin are only listed, with no detailed information included. Instead, some of the less conspicuous but brilliantly colored birds are presented, such as the Scarlet Tanager. Other species were selected because they illustrate an important ecological event (e.g., the warblers and their annual migration to the Southern Hemisphere) that has to be recognized and understood to assure the long-term health of the environment. Some species, such as the Serviceberry, were selected because they are conspicuous plants for a short time, yet few people know their names. Other species were selected to illustrate an important ecological concept, such as the Red-eyed Vireo, a bird that occupies a specific place in the forest structure. The presentation of a broad sampling of diverse species is designed to make it easier for the user to recognize different species and to develop a deeper understanding of the ecological mechanisms that are operating across the Tug Hill landscape.

Species are presented in four ways: they are featured in the *Narrative* at the beginning of each section, they appear in the *Illustrations*, they are explored in *Facts, Tips, and Lore*, or they are listed in the *Species Lists*. All the species featured in the *Narrative* are illustrated, and some are explored in more detail in *Facts, Tips, and Lore*. Species that seem to be most interesting were given the greatest attention and may appear in all four places. Not all of the species that are covered in *Facts, Tips, and Lore* are illustrated. To field identify those species not illustrated refer to the *Bibliography* for a specialized guide.

QUICK HABITAT FINDER GUIDE

The color-coded directory just inside the front cover will quickly guide the experienced user directly to the 10 sections that cover the major habitats. A brief description of each habitat is included to aid the inexperienced user in the initial identification of habitats.

COLOR-CODED EDGE BAND

Each section is marked on the page edges with a different color corresponding with the color band in the *Quick Habitat Finder Guide*. Once you make a preliminary identification of a habitat, use the color-coded edge band to find the section of the guide that describes that habitat and shows the species of plants and animals you are most likely to find there. Within the color-coded edge band is a symbol representing the subject type covered in that section.

VERIFYING CHARACTERISTICS

At the beginning of each section there is a detailed description of the components of the habitat covered. Use this description to verify the preliminary identification once you have entered the habitat.

NARRATIVE

The *Narrative* that follows the *Verifying Characteristics* highlights several species and events that can be experienced in the habitat, and is divided according to the seasons. Some superlative events are described and some remarkable species are discussed. The names of the species are in bold text to assist in locating a discussion of a particular species. Read this narrative at home to prepare you for field trips at the appropriate time and place to catch the spectacles presented.

ILLUSTRATIONS

The species of plants and animals most likely to be found in each habitat are grouped and illustrated on the color-coded pages following the narrative. Hints on how to find and identify each species within the habitat accompany each illustration. In the illustrations that include a background scene, those species that occupy a particular niche are shown in their proper setting. Some of the species are illustrated separately with a special painting or drawing.

MOST DISTINGUISHING CHARACTERISTICS

The viewpoints and the parts of a subject chosen for illustration were selected to show the easiest and most reliable clues for identification in the best season. A red arrow pointing to a feature in the illustration indicates the characteristic of the species that is the best clue to its identification.

FACTS, TIPS, AND LORE

For many species, a paragraph in the *Facts, Tips, and Lore* section provides more clues to assist in location and identification, or presents some biological or historical facts. This section is a *potpourri* of interesting information about selected species.

SPECIES LISTS

The *Species Lists* of trees, shrubs, mammals, birds, amphibians, and reptiles include most of the species that can be found on Tug Hill, listed alphabetically by the common name and followed by the scientific name. The list of herbaceous plants is extensive but not all-inclusive. Identification of the grass-like plants, the mosses, and the ferns is in many cases difficult even for the experts, so only an abbreviated list has been included. Insects are so diverse and specialized that they can only be listed by large taxonomic groupings. Those species featured in the *Guide* are shown in bold type on the list.

INDEX

Once you have determined from the Species Lists that a species is included in the *Guide*, refer to the index to find its location. The species listed in the index are only those species that are featured in the

Narrative, the *Illustrations,* or *Facts, Tips, and Lore.*

NOMENCLATURE

Common names are used to label species. For those species that are known by several common names, the name used locally is favored. In some cases, other common names that are widely used follow the primary common name in parentheses. The genus and species names used by scientists are given in the *Species List.*

MEASUREMENTS

Many sources were used to determine the dimensions shown on the illustrations, including reference books, direct observation, and the combined experiences of the writers. The dimensions given are those that seem to be the most useful to the casual naturalist. For example, the length of a bird is its length in a natural perching position, rather than the scientific method of measuring a specimen from the tip of its beak to the tip of its tail.

In the case of trees, shrubs, and herbaceous plants tree height, leaf length, and stalk height vary. The range given in these cases is an average of typical specimens.

WARNING

Plants that are noted to be edible or used for medicinal purposes are derived from folklore and historical accounts only. It is not recommended that any plant be used for personal consumption or medicinal purposes without consulting experts for proper identification and use.

MORE INFORMATION

The *Bibliography* lists several sources of information that are available to aid identification of species. Choose a book that specializes in the subject to explore a particular type of species in depth and compare related specimens.

GENERALIZED TUG HILL HABITATS (COVER TYPES)

FARMLANDS

HARDWOOD FORESTS, MIXED HARDWOODS AND SOFTWOODS, REFORESTED LANDS

SUCCESSIONAL FORESTS, SHRUBLANDS

WOODED SWAMPS, MARSHES AND WET MEADOWS, BEAVER FLOWS AND CREEKS (*Includes GULFS AND BOGS*)

DEVELOPED LANDS (*Not included in the Guide*)

TUG HILL HABITATS

HABITAT DESCRIPTIONS

The habitats named in this guide are variable, but they have certain characteristics that make each visually distinct from the others. The categorization generally follows the New York Natural Heritage Program's publication *"Ecological Communities of New York State"*. The names in parentheses are the closest Natural Heritage Program ecological communities. The paragraphs that follow list some of the species and associations that make the habitats distinct.

Hardwood Forests (Beech-maple mesic forest)

This habitat is dominated by Sugar Maple and American Beech, but other trees may include American Basswood, White Ash, Yellow Birch, Black Cherry, Red Maple, and Northern Red Oak. Among the relatively few shrubs and herbaceous plants are Striped Maple, Common Witchhazel, and Blue Cohosh.

Mixed Hardwoods and Softwoods (Hemlock-northern hardwood forest)

This habitat can contain all of the species of the Hardwood Forest, as well as scattered individual Eastern White Pines and Eastern Hemlocks, and some dense stands of Eastern Hemlock, Red Spruce, Balsam Fir, and Northern White Cedar. Small trees and shrubs include species of viburnum and blueberry. Herbaceous plants include Canada Mayflower and Bunchberry.

Successional Forests (Successional northern hardwoods)

This is a variable habitat, but the dominant trees are usually Quaking Aspen, Bigtooth Aspen, Black Cherry, Red Maple, White Pine, or Gray Birch. Openings and edges are often occupied by shrubland and farmland species.

Shrublands (Successional shrublands)

This habitat is a temporary stage in the natural reforestation of a cleared site, having at least 50% shrub cover. Shrubs include Gray Dogwood, raspberries, and species of viburnum. Openings between shrub masses are often occupied by herbaceous species, such as Common Milkweed and species of goldenrod.

Farmlands (Cropland/field crops)

This is an open habitat occupied by an ever-changing cover of row crops and hay, as well as pasture land and fallow fields. Field edges and uncultivated spaces are often occupied by non-native species, including Queen-Anne's-Lace and Common Mullein. Hedgerows include mixed tree species from forest and successional habitats.

Reforested Lands (Pine, Spruce/fir plantation)

This habitat consists of straight, evenly spaced rows of softwood trees planted for the cultivation and harvest of timber products, or for erosion control. Species can include Eastern White Pine, Red Pine, Scotch Pine, White Spruce, and Balsam Fir.

Wooded Swamps (Red maple-hardwood swamp, Hemlock-hardwood swamp)

This is a low-lying, periodically wet forest habitat dominated by Red Maple, Eastern Hemlock, or Tamarack. The herbaceous layer is often dominated by ferns.

Marshes and Wet Meadows (Shallow or Deep emergent marsh, Rich graminoid fen)

This permanently wet habitat is dominated by grasses and sedges. Cattail and species of waterlily may be present , as well as masses of shrubs, such as Leatherleaf or Sheep Laurel.

Beaver Flows and Creeks (Rocky headwater stream, Marsh headwater stream)

This habitat is found along flowing water or a ponded section of a stream. Shrubs along the edge and in the floodplain include Speckled Alder and Common Elderberry. Old beaver flows are often occupied by Boneset and Cardinal-flower.

Gulfs and Bogs (Shale cliff and talus, Dwarf shrub bog)

These habitats are uncommon and isolated and may contain some species of plants that are not likely to be found in any other habitat.

Crown
The leafy top of an individual tree

Canopy
The intermeshed tops of the tallest trees

Understory
The scattered crowns of shade-tolerant small trees and shrubs

Den Tree
A tree, alive or dead, that shelters wildlife

Sapling
A young individual of a tree species

Shrub Layer
Zone of shrub growth, height varies from 6" to 25'

Pit and Mound
Small depression accompanied by a mound

Herbaceous/ Fern Layer
Annual & Perennial plants, height varies from 1" - 6'

Seedling
An emerging tree

Forest Floor
The ground beneath the trees

Windthrow
A tree blown over by the wind, having its roots tipped into the air

Duff Layer
The accumulated organic matter on the forest floor

VISUAL GLOSSARY

Photo by Robert McNamara

THE REGION

Travel on Route 81 toward Watertown, follow Route 12 along sharp east-facing slopes through Turin, look north from the Madison County hills, or look east from the shores of Lake Ontario. The conspicuous high ground on the horizon is Tug Hill. Tug Hill is an extensive elevated region with a comparatively flat surface that descends, abruptly in places, to the surrounding lowlands. The landform has a distinct appearance and fascinating geologic history.

Tug Hill is bordered by the Lake Ontario lowlands to the west, the Mohawk Valley to the south, and the Black River Valley to the north and east. The highest elevation reaches 2,100 feet, high above the valley floors and surrounding lake plains whose elevations are about 300 feet. The average elevation of the broad upland on top of Tug Hill is about 1,800 feet.

The forces that created the landform that we see today would make for an awesome spectacle if you could watch from a satellite, and time could be compressed from 450 million years to 24 hours. During the first hour you would be looking down upon a vast sea that covered the entire region during Ordovician times. Corals, bryozoans, crinoids, snails, starfish, trilobites, nautiloids, brachiopods, and a multitude of other life forms live and die in the sea. Many of these creatures extract elements from the water to make their shells. They die and collect on the ocean floor in deeper and deeper layers, compressing those below until they consolidate, crystallize, and transform into the limestone rock of the Black River and Trenton Groups.

As time passes, uplifts of land occur in what is now New England, and mountains are thrust above sea level. Mountain ranges are attacked by erosion as streams transport mud, silt, and sand westward. Deltas form on the margins of the sea and near-shore deposits are transported by currents, blanketing limey off-shore deposits of what now make up the Black River and Trenton limestones. These deposits cover and intermingle with deeper water sediments and transform into the Oswego sandstones and the sandstones, siltstones, and shales of the Lorraine Group. Some sediments are deposited in stagnant waters where organic material is only partially decomposed. These sediments become the black colored Utica shale. Brachiopods, trilobites, graptolites, and nautiloids fossilize in the black shale. Some fossils are replaced by iron-sulfur compounds, forming pyrite. The presence of few fossils may be attributed to the stagnant bottom conditions. The petroleum odor from unweathered fragments of rock may be attributed to organic remains chemically altered by bacterial action in a stagnant environment.

As time ticks away and hours pass, spectacular geologic events occur. Our realization of these events is obscured. Millions of years of rock are not accounted for today because they have been worn away by erosion.

In the 24th hour the action intensifies. Within the last 6 minutes (about 2 million years ago), the climate turns colder and enormous ice sheets form in the north. Several advances and retreats of these ice sheets modify the landscape.

The final glacial advance occurs during the last 6 seconds of our racing clock (about 30,000 years ago). As the ice advances from the north, it gouges and scours the surface, deepening and widening valleys and planing off hilltops. The ice plucks away bedrock masses weighing up to several tons. Such plucking and scouring carves the softer layers of the Trenton Group more deeply than the solid limestone layers, leaving step-like escarpments rising from lowlands along the flanks of Tug Hill.

The glacier advances and plasters the bedrock surface with rock debris. Some of it is carried many miles from the north, which explains the presence of foreign boulders called *erratics*. The ice builds to a thickness of several thousand feet, depressing the earth's crust beneath.

The climate warms and the last of the glacial ice melts and retreats in the last 2 seconds (about 10,000 years ago), leaving a veneer of unsorted rock debris (*glacial till*). Till blankets the land, some having been molded deep below the ice as *drumlins* (hills shaped like upside-down spoons) oriented parallel with the direction of glacier movement. Some till is left in mounds and winding ridges at points where the advancing glacier stagnates. Other features composed of sorted sands and gravels are deposited as mounds and terraces because the till is rearranged by melt water.

As glaciers continue to retreat, water from huge ancestral Great Lakes discharges into Lake Iroquois (ancestral Lake Ontario). Waves of Lake Iroquois lap against Tug Hill, ravaging glacial deposits and spreading them as sandy beaches, cobble-strewn beaches, and off shore bars.

(These features may be seen along Routes 11 and 81 along the west side of the Hill). Rivers of meltwater surge through the Mohawk and Hudson Valleys and on to the sea. As ice retreats further north, a drainage passage opens in the St. Lawrence region. In the last seconds, as the climate continues to warm, Lake Iroquois shrinks to a small remnant of its former size (present day Lake Ontario).

Glacially scoured valleys and other depressions filled with sand and gravel are saturated with water. These deposits, flanking the western and southwestern margins of the Hill, serve as valuable reservoirs for ground water storage (the Tug Hill Aquifer).

Numerous wetlands fill the glacially scoured depressions and abandoned glacial stream channels on the relatively flat top of Tug Hill. Others fill basins in morainic features that collect water and impede its percolation. The water table rises from the heavy rain and snow that falls on the Hill.

Runoff from melting snow and rain collects through irregularly branched tributaries that join into a main channel, a *dendritic pattern* (resembling the branches of a tree). The streams rush over the steep margins of Tug Hill, cutting through resistant sandstones and into softer siltstones and shales. As streams cut back into the Hill, downward erosion speeds up. Deep, narrow gorges are formed (gulfs). Rock debris tumbling down valley walls is carried by streams and eventually deposited as fine soil on flood plains.

Fine soil and abundant moisture allows vegetation to quickly invade from the south. Mosses, lichens, and grasses at first but then shrubs and pioneer trees move up from the valleys. Some cold-hardy trees from high elevations spring up on top of the Hill and some warm climate species from the south also form stands. The resulting mix is considered a transition community between the boreal forest of Canada and the temperate forest of the Allegheny Plateau. The plants flourish in the abundant moisture, the colors and textures change as the pioneer species are replaced by trees that can grow in their own shade (*the climax forest*).

Insects abound, birds fly in, and wolves, bears, panthers, and moose roam through the trees. Diverse habitat *niches* (specific portions of the cover or food supply available in a larger habitat type) fill and establish equilibrium. The action slows and stability reigns.

The first Europeans, who came in from Lake Ontario and up the

Mohawk River, were greeted by a seemingly endless reservoir of water, mineral, forest, and wildlife resources. Today the region is still rich with many of the same assets that attracted the original settlers.

PART TWO
UPLANDS

Lucky Break - White-tailed Deer

Painting by Robert McNamara

HARDWOOD FORESTS

VERIFYING CHARACTERISTICS

- Little Understory
- Seedlings Same Species as Canopy
- Ground Carpeted with Leaves
- Pits and Mounds on Forest Floor

"We've got an area here that is unique.
It's a plateau, a unique area of lands,
forests, and streams. The entire Tug Hill
region represents the history of settlement
in the north country"

John Constable, Jr.

Enter the Tug Hill hardwood forest, a mature component of the Great Northern Forest, a landscape the Northern Forest Lands Council describes as one of the largest expanses of continuously forested land in the nation. This forest type was once called the Beech-Birch-Maple Forest, but it has been renamed the Beech-Maple Mesic Forest by the New York Natural Heritage Program. A *mesic forest* is a forest that is growing on moist, well-drained soils. The farmer knows this forest as the *sugarbush* and the logger knows it as the *woodlot*. You may be quite familiar with this habitat, but have you ever taken a close look?

The silence of the hardwood forest disguises the production that is going on all around you. Every living thing is cycling in a state of dynamic equilibrium from the ground to the trees to the ground again. Nothing is wasted. Nothing is unnecessary. When a tree dies it becomes host to a multitude of organisms, from bacteria to the Pileated Woodpecker, all harvesting products to sustain their lives and, in turn, making nutrients available to other life forms.

We can benefit from the productivity of the forest by harvesting products like lumber and firewood, and, if managed properly, the forest will continually renew itself. In some cases, however, preservation or management for wilderness characteristics is appropriate to maintain the intangible values of wilderness as a source of inspiration and

19

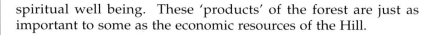

spiritual well being. These 'products' of the forest are just as important to some as the economic resources of the Hill.

The forest you are looking at has undergone many changes since the first settlers came to Tug Hill. The settlers found a primeval forest made up of plant communities that had evolved to a state of climax following the retreat of the Wisconsin Glacier around 10,000 years ago. The activities of people in the intervening years have changed the mosaic of plant communities on the Hill. The spruce-fir forest, once more extensive, has declined and the hardwood and the successional forests have advanced. The hardwoods have probably been harvested several times since the initial cutting, yet the forest remains productive. The changes have been detrimental to some species such as the wolf, lynx, and moose, while they have favored others like the coyote, deer, and certain migratory songbirds.

If well managed, a new equilibrium can be achieved, balancing the needs of the people and the environment. New communities could be managed to provide a sustained yield of timber products, wildlife resources, agriculture, and recreation.

Spring

Maple sugaring time signals the loss of winter's grip and the rebirth of dormant life. While we are collecting the sap for fun and profit, Red Squirrels lap the sweet liquid from tree wounds, and on warm days, insects congregate around the spiles and buckets.

There are many performances in the forest that are a treat to experience, but you have to be in the right place at the right time. In the spring, as the snow pack is melting, before the leaves break out of bud, wildflowers take advantage of the free look at the sun and bloom in colorful profusion. In some places *Showy Trilliums* carpet the forest floor with a white display that is hard to miss. Other flowers, such as the *Jack-in-the-pulpit*, require a little searching. The subtle greenish-brown colors and concealing hood of the Jack-in-the-pulpit hide its curious flower parts.

Take advantage of the missing leaves and look up to the canopy for migrating warblers, resident vireos, the most common bird of the canopy, and the brilliant male *Scarlet Tanager*. Spring offers the best opportunity to see his striking scarlet flash through the trees, since soon the buds will break and the trees will leaf out. The male tanager sings in the treetops, proclaiming its territory and advertising for a mate. Once the birds have mated and nested they will fall silent, and will seldom venture from the upper branches of the trees. The tanager and some other migratory birds have declined, probably from loss of habitat on their tropical wintering grounds and *fragmentation* (subdivision of large forests into smaller pieces by roadbuilding and clearing) of habitat on the breeding grounds. Tanagers and other songbirds are also vulnerable to *nest predation* (intrusion on the nest of one species by another) by the **Brown-headed Cowbird**, a bird with an unusual method of reproduction. The cowbird lays its eggs in the nests of other birds. When the cowbird eggs hatch the chicks push the host chicks out of the nest and the host adults unknowingly raise the intruders. Fragmentation allows the cowbird to penetrate to the forest core and parasitize the tanager and other forest dwelling birds. Development, such as homebuilding, farming, and harvesting forest products changes the species composition of the forest, benefiting a few species while causing many others to decrease in number.

Brown-headed Cowbird

Come back in the evening for a different treat. Woodland amphibians migrate to *vernal pools* (temporary pools in low areas) to breed and deposit their eggs. The young hatch, mature, and then disperse into the forest before the pools dry up. The temporary nature of the pools prevents establishment of other species, such as fishes, that might feed on the amphibian eggs and young. Although temporary, the pools are crucial to the survival of some species.

The shrill whistle of the **Spring Peeper** and the duck-like croaks of the **Wood Frog** will lead you to the pools. The resonance of the peeper's song makes it difficult to pinpoint its location, a mechanism of defense. To find a peeper, try locating the source of the sound from a distance, then move forward, crouch by the site and hold still. You can see the tiny frog inflate its bubblegum-thin throat to make a sound you would never expect to come from such a small creature. A single frog will start a chorus, then another will join, and another until the sound is almost deafening. Make a move and all will be silent again. The Wood Frog is the first amphibian to make an appearance on Tug Hill each year. It is called the *Robber Frog* by some because of the mask-like patch of black across its eyes. If you are lucky enough to be in the right place at the right time you may hear the choruses of Spring Peepers and Wood Frogs alternate, then intermix in a spring nighttime serenade.

Near the pools look for **Spotted Salamanders** as you listen to alternating waves of dueling frog choruses. The Spotted Salamander spends most of its time in the damp darkness of decomposing leaves and wood, feeding on earthworms. In early spring it leaves its winter retreat and migrates overland to the pool where it was born, sometimes in congregations of hundreds of individuals. The male courts a female underwater and if it is successful it deposits a *spermatophore* (a small package of sperm) on the pool bottom. The female picks it up and fertilization takes place. She releases eggs in clusters of up to 200 and glues them to underwater twigs. Look for greenish gelatinous masses just below the surface of the water. The green color is the result of a *symbiotic relationship* (an association that benefits both) between the eggs and an algae. The algae lives off the jelly in the egg mass, receives carbon dioxide from the developing eggs, and in turn supplies the developing embryos with vital oxygen. In about 45 days, the eggs hatch and the salamanders exist as larvae, feeding on tiny pond animals. Larvae usually *metamorphose* (change form) into adults by the end of summer, though some may winter in the immature phase. A simple puddle can be a fascinating place.

Watch for a dark streak overhead. You may be surrounded by flying creatures with big black eyes. As the weather warms the **Southern Flying Squirrel** emerges from its den in a Pileated Woodpecker hole or other tree cavity to feed under the cover of night. The Southern Flying Squirrel cannot really fly; it glides or drops in a prolonged and controlled fall, using outstretched membranes attached at the wrists and ankles. The squirrel launches itself from a high tree, glides through the darkness to a nearby tree, scampers up a little higher, and then takes off again for another 'flight', using its flat tail as a rudder for mid-course corrections. Though secretive, the Southern Flying Squirrel is more numerous in the forest than the familiar Gray Squirrel.

Summer

Leaves have burst forth from the buds in a spurt of growth that seems miraculous. Compare the leaves of different trees to take the first steps toward identification. A leaf can be *simple* (an individual leaf on a stem), or *compound* (several leaflets along each side of a stem). It can be arranged opposite another leaf on a twig, at alternate locations along the twig, or in whorls around the twig. The margin may be smooth, lobed, or toothed. These characteristics are the primary identifiers used in most identification keys.

In summer the canopy closes and the inhabitants disappear into the lush greenery, taking advantage of the cover to nest and rear young. Early summer is the time for a proliferation of insects, coincident with the nesting activities of birds. Insects are abundant, feeding on foliage, tunneling, boring, depositing eggs, and searching for the blood of mammals. Summer in the hardwood forest is the domain of the mosquito. Protect yourself from the pests, but recognize the importance of such an abundant food source to the birds nesting there.

Watch for birds carrying food to locate their nests, but observe them from a distance. Raccoons and other predators will follow the scent of people; they have learned that the path usually leads to food, so do not go near a nest. Once you determine the repetitious path of feeding birds, it is possible to be ready for a good look or even a photograph.

Late in the day the darkening forest trills with a melancholy flute-like song echoing through the understory. Thrushes make these melodious calls. The **Wood Thrush** is the most common, and its song is a soothing and peaceful tribute to the stability of the hardwood forest.

Fall

Smell the pungent odors that waft from the *forest duff* (the decaying organic layer next to the soil) and take in the explosion of color on the changing trees. Fall is a treat for the senses and the northern hardwood forest is the place to be during this fleeting season. As the leaves are dropping you can once again see through the tree crowns and spot migrating warblers.

Watch the carpet of leaves and needles for other movements. It will not be long before a **Wolf Spider** or a Harvestman (*Daddy Longlegs*) comes along. The Daddy Longlegs makes a living by capturing tiny insects, scavenging dead organisms, or sucking plant juices. In our region, the Wolf Spider is probably the most feared spider because it is big and hairy, like a tarantula, and it moves fast. It is probably of little comfort, but both the Wolf Spiders and the Daddy Longlegs are harmless to people. The Wolf Spider is active day and night, as it hunts for insect prey. A female Wolf Spider lays its eggs in a spherical sac of silk that it carries around until the young hatch. The young spiders remain with their mother for a time, crawling over her body as she moves. At some point, the young Wolf Spiders spin a strand of silk that catches air currents as it pays out. The young spiders drift off on this balloon of silk to find a place to settle.

Winter

Winter is the season for which Tug Hill is most famous. Snow blankets the forest floor and triggers various survival mechanisms in most species. Loggers find winter the best time of year to harvest forest products without damaging streams or wet places and without coating the logs with mud.

Study the branching habits, bark textures, buds, and seeds of trees. These identifiers are as reliable as leaf shapes are in summer. Locate the **Common Witchhazel** by looking for crown-like seed capsules on one of the few understory trees found in the hardwood forest. The seed capsules pop when mature and can eject a seed up to 20 feet. Flowers with thread-like yellow petals can still be on the plants when there is snow on the ground in November.

Some inhabitants are easiest to find during winter. Listen for heavy, thudding blows on a hollow tree in 13 beat groups. A **Pileated Woodpecker** is proclaiming its territory. You may be able to catch a glimpse of the bird as it flies from tree to tree. The Pileated Woodpecker drills nesting holes in live and dead trees. The abandoned holes often become dens for other species such as squirrels or owls. Study the holes for recent scratch marks, and look on the ground below the hole for evidence of occupation, then wait patiently for some activity. Trees with cavities that are likely to house wildlife should be left standing for their habitat value, whether they are dead or alive.

All seems dead in winter, but all you have to do is stop and be quiet. As you crunch through the snow you warn the creatures of approaching danger, but when you stop and hold still for a minute, activity resumes. Watch for woodpeckers hopping up dead branches in search of food.

Winter is the best season to search the snow for a record of the activities of the inhabitants of the hardwood forest. Follow the tracks and discover the habits, shelters, and food sources of woodland mammals. Examine *scat* (animal droppings) for clues on diet.

On sunny winter days when the temperature climbs above freezing, look closely at depressions in the snow; they may appear peppered with little black spots. Hold your hand close to the ground by a group of the specks and you will soon be holding several energetic jumpers. The specks are **Snow Fleas** feeding on algae growing in the snow. Magnify them with a hand lens or look backward through your binoculars and you might get a better look at the grotesque little insects than you had wanted. Snow Fleas are not actually fleas and they do not really jump. They are members of a primitive order of insects called *Springtails* that move by catapulting themselves into the air.

ILLUSTRATIONS

Sugar Maple
*Max. height to 125',
common 75'-100'*

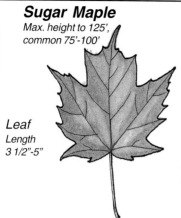

Leaf
*Length
3 1/2"-5"*

Fruit *A pair of
winged seeds*

Bark *Mature trunk
shown, young bark
smooth to 6" dia.*

Twig & Bud
*Buds opposite,
twigs glossy*

American Beech
*Max. height to 120',
common 60'-80'*

Leaf
*Length
2 1/2"-6"*

Fruit *3/4" long,
2 triangular seeds
per husk*

Bark *Trunk & limbs
permanently smooth,
often blotched*

Twig & Bud
*Buds sharp
pointed*

Yellow Birch
*Max. height to 100',
common 50'-70'*

Leaf
*Length
3"-4 1/2"*

Fruit *1 1/4"
long,
cone-like*

Bark *Lustrous,
peeling into
ribbon-like strips*

Twig & Bud
*Twig has
wintergreen
flavor*

Black Cherry
*Max. height to 90',
common 40'-60'*

Leaf
*Length
2"-5"*

Fruit *Aug.-
Oct. 3/8" dia.*

Bark *Mature bark
shown, young bark
satiny reddish-brown*

Twig & Bud
Buds alternate

Leaf
Length
5"-9"

Acorn
3/4" long,
with flat,
shallow cup

**Twig &
Bud**
Buds
clustered

Northern Red Oak
Max. height to 100'
common 50'-80'

Bark Smooth
when young, flat-
ridged later

Leaf
Length
4"-9"

Acorn
3/4" long,
with deep,
bowl-shaped cup

**Twig &
Bud** Buds
globular

White Oak
Max. height to 100'
common 60'-80'

Bark Fissured
with scaly ridges

Leaf
Length
8"-12",
7 leaflets

Fruit
1"-2" long,
in clusters

**Twig &
Bud** Buds
opposite

White Ash
Height 60'-80'

Bark
Regularly fissured

Leaf
Length
5"-7"

Fruit
Each wing
1" long,

Bark
Green & White
stripes give the
tree its name

**Twig &
Bud** Buds
opposite

Striped Maple
Max. height 40', common 5'-15'

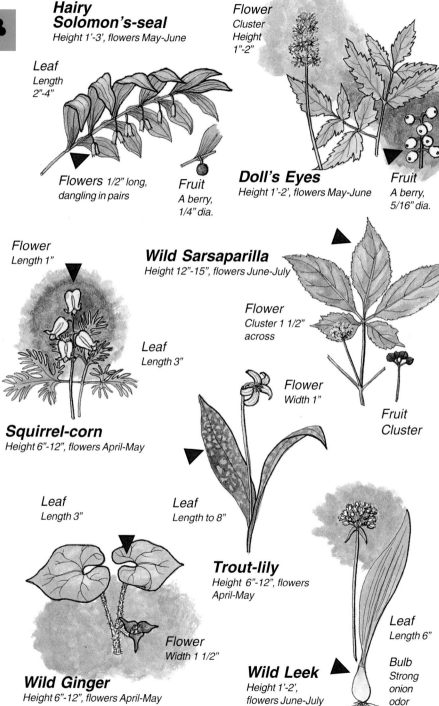

Hairy Solomon's-seal
Height 1'-3', flowers May-June

Leaf
Length
2"-4"

Flowers 1/2" long,
dangling in pairs

Fruit
A berry,
1/4" dia.

Flower
Cluster
Height
1"-2"

Doll's Eyes
Height 1'-2', flowers May-June

Fruit
A berry,
5/16" dia.

Flower
Length 1"

Squirrel-corn
Height 6"-12", flowers April-May

Wild Sarsaparilla
Height 12"-15", flowers June-July

Leaf
Length 3"

Flower
Cluster 1 1/2"
across

Flower
Width 1"

Fruit
Cluster

Leaf
Length 3"

Leaf
Length to 8"

Trout-lily
Height 6"-12", flowers
April-May

Flower
Width 1 1/2"

Wild Ginger
Height 6"-12", flowers April-May

Wild Leek
Height 1'-2',
flowers June-July

Leaf
Length 6"

Bulb
Strong
onion
odor

Blue Cohosh
Height 1'-3', flowers May-June

Leaf
Length 6"

Flower
Cluster height 1 1/2"

Fruit
*Cluster of berries,
each 3/8" dia.*

Flower
Width 3"

Wake Robin
*Height 8"-16",
flowers April-May*

Leaf
Length to 6"

Flower
Width 3"

Leaf
Length to 6"

Showy Trillium
Height 1'-1 1/2', flowers April-May

Flower
Width 2"

Leaf
Length to 4"

**Painted
Trillium**
*Height 8"-20",
flowers April-May*

Flower
Length 3"

Jack-in-the-pulpit
Height 8"-18", flowers April-May

Leaf
Length 5"

Flower
Width 3/4"

Flower
Width 1"

Flower
Width 3/4"

Leaf
Length to 6"

Bloodroot
*Height 6"-14",
flowers April-May*

Leaf
Length to 8"

Carolina Spring Beauty
Height 2"-4", flowers April-May

Leaf
Length 2"

**Sharp-lobed
Hepatica**
*Height 4"-6", flowers
March-April*

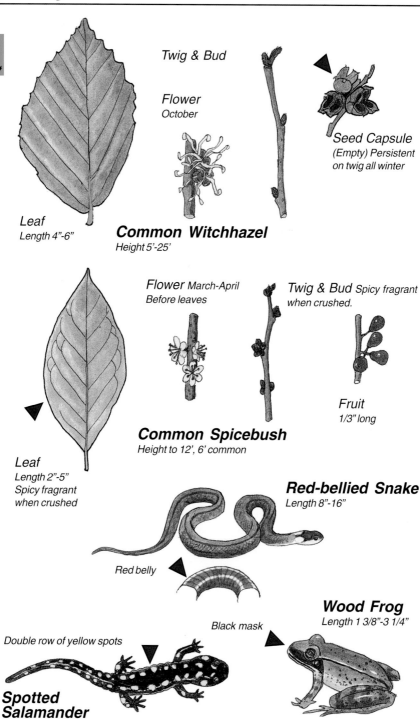

Twig & Bud

Flower
October

Seed Capsule
*(Empty) Persistent
on twig all winter*

Leaf
Length 4"-6"

Common Witchhazel
Height 5'-25'

Flower March-April
Before leaves

Twig & Bud *Spicy fragrant
when crushed.*

Fruit
1/3" long

Common Spicebush
Height to 12', 6' common

Leaf
*Length 2"-5"
Spicy fragrant
when crushed*

Red-bellied Snake
Length 8"-16"

Red belly

Wood Frog
Length 1 3/8"-3 1/4"

Black mask

Double row of yellow spots

Spotted
Salamander
Length 6"-9 3/4"

Eastern Chipmunk
Body 5"- 6", Tail 3"- 4"

Gray Squirrel
Body 10"-11", Tail 10"-12"

1 1/8"

2 1/4"

Red-backed Vole
Body 3 2/3"- 4 2/3", Tail 1 1/5"- 2"

Tail Drag Mark

3/4"

1 1/2"

Southern Flying Squirrel
Body 5 1/2"- 5 2/3",
Tail 3 1/2"- 4 1/2"

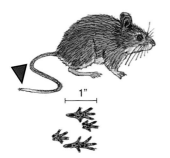

1"

Woodland Jumping Mouse
Body 3 3/5"- 4", Tail 5"- 6 1/5"

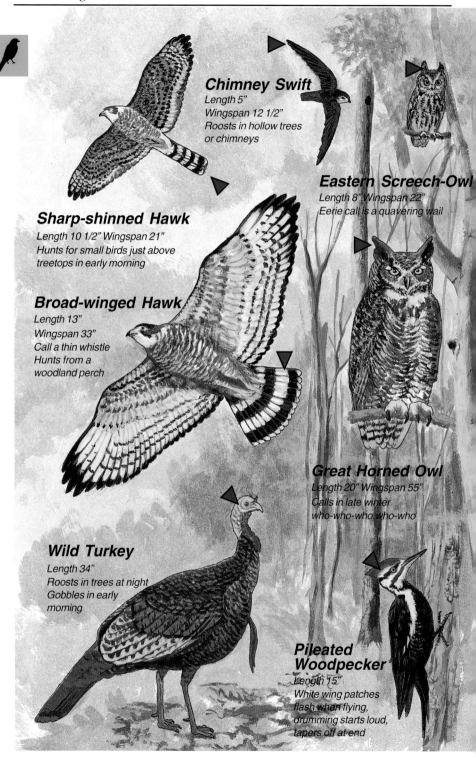

Chimney Swift
Length 5"
Wingspan 12 1/2"
Roosts in hollow trees
or chimneys

Eastern Screech-Owl
Length 8" Wingspan 22"
Eerie call is a quavering wail

Sharp-shinned Hawk
Length 10 1/2" Wingspan 21"
Hunts for small birds just above
treetops in early morning

Broad-winged Hawk
Length 13"
Wingspan 33"
Call a thin whistle
Hunts from a
woodland perch

Great Horned Owl
Length 20" Wingspan 55"
Calls in late winter
who-who-who,who-who

Wild Turkey
Length 34"
Roosts in trees at night
Gobbles in early
morning

Pileated Woodpecker
Length 15"
White wing patches
flash when flying,
drumming starts loud,
tapers off at end

Red-eyed Vireo
Length 5"
Most common bird in the canopy, sings continuously

Great Crested Flycatcher
Length 7"
Listen for loud, raspy wheep from treetops

Scarlet Tanager
Length 6 1/4"
Brilliant red, feeding and singing in treetops

Brown Creeper
Length 4 3/4"
Tiny bird, blends in with bark, listen for high, faint peeping, look for spiral feeding action around tree trunk

Downy Woodpecker
Length 5 3/4"
Common, smaller than Hairy, small bill

Hairy Woodpecker
Length 7 1/2"
Large bill, robin size body

Veery
Length 6"
Found in vegetation on the forest floor

Wood Thrush
Length 7"
Sings a melancholy flute-like song from understory at dusk

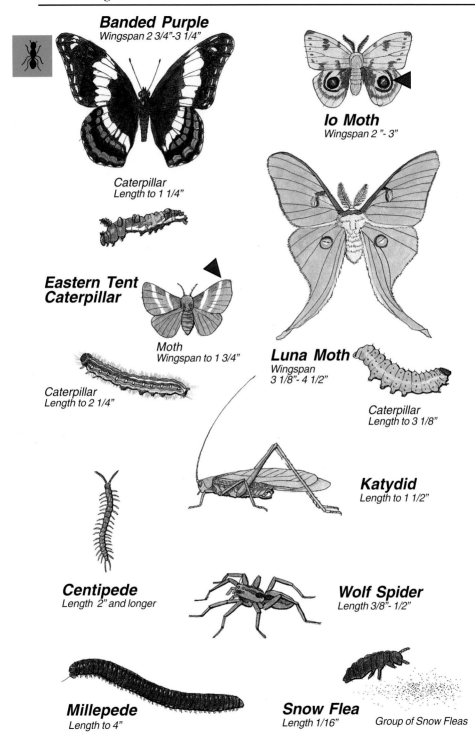

Banded Purple
Wingspan 2 3/4"-3 1/4"

Io Moth
Wingspan 2 "- 3"

Caterpillar
Length to 1 1/4"

Eastern Tent Caterpillar

Moth
Wingspan to 1 3/4"

Caterpillar
Length to 2 1/4"

Luna Moth
Wingspan 3 1/8"- 4 1/2"

Caterpillar
Length to 3 1/8"

Katydid
Length to 1 1/2"

Centipede
Length 2" and longer

Wolf Spider
Length 3/8"- 1/2"

Millepede
Length to 4"

Snow Flea
Length 1/16"   *Group of Snow Fleas*

FACTS, TIPS, AND LORE

FACTS, TIPS, *AND* LORE
HARDWOOD FORESTS

TREES

American Beech

The smooth bark of the beech invites carving, but please resist. The open wounds let in diseases that can kill the tree. A deadly fungus currently threatens the beech. The high crotches of old trees are a good place to look for raptor nests. The triangular nuts are edible, but better if roasted. Many species of birds and mammals eat beechnuts.

White Oak

In the past, White Oak was used for wet cooperage because pores in the wood are impervious to liquids. It was also prized for shipbuilding. Today White Oak is used in the building industry for floors, cabinets, and trim. The acorns of this and other oaks are an extremely valuable winter food source for many wildlife species.

Northern Red Oak

In the past, Red Oak could only be used for dry cooperage because the wood is porous. It was also used for many other products from boxes to agricultural implements. It is still used today for flooring and other construction and industrial products. Trees are usually widely scattered, except in a few places in the southern part of Tug Hill where soil conditions favor oaks over the other hardwoods.

Black Cherry

Cherry is prized for fine furniture, and it is perhaps the most valuable timber species on the Hill. The fruit is also a favorite of many species of mammals and birds. Rodents especially treasure the seeds and pack them away in any convenient cache, such as the air filters and exhaust pipes of logging equipment. Cherries are covered with tent caterpillar nests and defoliated by the caterpillars during cyclical population surges, but the infestation is seldom fatal to the tree.

Sugar Maple (Hard Maple)

This maple is probably the most recognized and useful tree on the Hill. It is also the state tree of New York. The sugarbush is the name given to almost any stand where maples are predominant, and sap from the trees is an important resource for farmers and occasional harvesters as well. Insects, squirrels, and birds also savor maple sap. The roadside rows of gnarled old maples are a trademark of scenic Tug Hill communities and are markers for communities that once were. Maple dieback (a general decline caused by air pollution and insect pests) is taking its toll on the old trees and the stately landmarks are disappearing. Young trees should be planted to get a start before the old sentinels are gone.

Yellow Birch

Campers know this tree for its shredded bark curls that are flammable even in the wettest weather. It was the source of wintergreen oil before the oil became artificially produced. This tree is often seen on 'legs', where a seedling got started on an old stump and the stump then rotted away. The wood is a favorite for veneer. Yellow Birch seeds provide food for finches, Pine Siskins, Redpolls, and other birds throughout the winter.

White Ash

White Ash is the last major tree to 'leaf out' in spring and the first to drop its leaves in fall. Ash wood is used for baseball bats and tool handles. When steamed and bent, it is used for snowshoe and dogsled frames.

Striped Maple

Striped Maple is a small understory tree seldom reaching 4 inches in trunk diameter. It is called Moosewood by some since moose feed on it, and Goosefoot by others because the leaves are shaped like the footprint of a goose. White-tailed Deer find it ideal for antler rubbing since it is usually growing in an area where predators can be seen. In spring dark 'soot' (fungal spores) covers the buds and will leave marks on your clothing that look like charcoal stripes.

SHRUBS

Common Spicebush

Spicebush is found in the understory of bottomland forests. This plant is the host for the striking Spicebush Swallowtail Butterfly. Look for the swallowtail caterpillar in a rolled leaf, or the chrysalis lashed to a twig with silken threads. The fruit of the spicebush has been used as a substitute for allspice.

Common Witchhazel

Witchhazel grows in the shady understory in a loose, open form with just a few stems. The plant has been used medicinally as a cure-all, and extracts can still be purchased. Native Americans made a tea-like drink from the leaves.

American Black Currant (not illustrated)

The tree farmer despises this shrub because it provides habitat for a stage in the life cycle of the fungus that causes White Pine Blister Rust, a disease that damages White Pine Trees. The fruit makes a good jelly and pie filling, but eradication programs make the plant hard to find.

HERBACEOUS PLANTS

Jack-in-the-Pulpit (Indian Turnip)

This plant is named for its flowering stalk (the Jack) and the overhanging leaf-like structure (the pulpit). Male and female plants are separate, therefore, the 'Jack' is either the male or female reproductive organ. Plants arise from a perennial underground root and in different years the same root may produce male or female plants. In the fall most of the plant withers away, except for the striking cluster of bright red berries. There are two varieties of Jack-in-the-pulpit in moist woods. The most common variety has a dark purplish and green pulpit, while the other is totally green. WARNING: Do not eat this plant raw because it contains calcium oxalate crystals, which can cause a strong burning sensation.

Bloodroot

The Bloodroot flowers appear early, before the showy leaves. Find the red root and scratch it to see the `blood' for which this plant was named. WARNING: Plant is poisonous.

Trout-Lily (Adder's Tongue, Dogtooth Violet)

The nodding flower of Trout-lily is one of the earliest treats of spring, sometimes blooming beside persistent patches of snow. The flowers move to follow the path of the sun and close at night.

Wake Robin, Showy Trillium, Painted Trillium

These three species of trillium are welcome sights in spring, but they are best left in the woods, not only because they are protected plants, but also because the smell of a bouquet inside your house is not nearly as pleasant as the sight of the flowers in the woods. The Showy Trillium often covers large areas of low, rich woods with a blanket of white flowers that fade to pink as they age. Mutants are occasionally found with green flowers. The Wake Robin is among the first flowers to bloom in spring. The Painted Trillium is the smallest of the three and is often found with the Wake Robin on higher ground.

Carolina Spring Beauty

Carolina Spring Beauty grows from small potato-like tubers that have a sweet chestnut-like flavor. Native Americans and colonists used them for food and even today they are still enjoyed by those interested in wild plants. In early spring, Tug Hill hardwood forests abound with this flower, but if you harvest it, do so sparingly. Wild Turkeys, White-tailed Deer, and many small mammals prize the tubers.

Sharp-lobed Hepatica (Liverwort)

Hepatica is also called Liverwort because of the shape, color, and mottling of its leaves. The color of the flowers can vary from white to pink, purple, or blue. At one time, the woods were scoured for this plant to be used as a liver remedy, but it has never been proven to have any medicinal value.

Wild Sarsaparilla

This plant is most easily noticed when it is flowering, and only then do you realize how common it is. Most of the time it is overlooked in the forest understory. The roots are very aromatic and run horizontally through the soil. They make a good summer drink, and were once used as a blood purifier. WARNING: Do not eat the berries as they contain a poisonous glycoside.

MOSSES and FERNS

Green Silk Moss (not illustrated)

This moss grows in the deciduous forest and can be a dominant plant in places. It is a robust moss that forms loose but hefty mats that are a pale green color. It is found on rocks, logs, surfaces above the leaf litter, and in shaded areas, often those that are dry or disturbed. In very early spring it is often the only green plant visible in the forest. This moss has been used for bedding, it has antibiotic properties, it repels insects, and it is rot resistant.

Interrupted Fern   (not illustrated)

This large, coarse fern was named for the fertile leaflets that grow along the stem in 4 or more pairs. Soon after these leaflets release the spores, they fall off, leaving an interruption in the regular leaflet pattern.

MAMMALS

Red-backed Vole

This vole does not tunnel, it wanders under the leaf litter of cool, shady woodlands. Unlike most of its relatives, this vole is active in broad daylight, feeding on leaves of low-growing plants, roots, insects, and beechnuts. The red color, unusual for a vole, serves as camouflage against the leaves and needles on the forest floor.

Eastern Chipmunk

Listen for a repetitive chirp in the fall forest, stalk toward the sound, and look for a quick movement on a downed log. Watch for the active

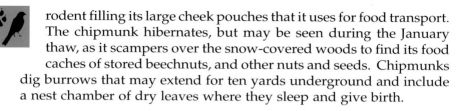

rodent filling its large cheek pouches that it uses for food transport. The chipmunk hibernates, but may be seen during the January thaw, as it scampers over the snow-covered woods to find its food caches of stored beechnuts, and other nuts and seeds. Chipmunks dig burrows that may extend for ten yards underground and include a nest chamber of dry leaves where they sleep and give birth.

Gray Squirrel

The Gray Squirrel is more common in the Oneida Lake Forest than in the Core Forest. Watch for this squirrel sneaking around the trunk of a tree or poking just its head out of a tree cavity den on a sunny winter day. Watch a Gray Squirrel as it gathers acorns, beechnuts, hickory nuts, walnuts, fruit, and fungi, or eats the bark off branches during winter and spring. This squirrel caches nuts singly in the ground, and tamps the soil down with its snout. During winter, a squirrel can relocate these nuts by smell, even through 10 inches of snow.

Woodland Jumping Mouse

This little mouse can regularly jump at least 8 feet. You may catch a glimpse of this forest rodent diving under fallen trees or logs where nests of shredded materials may be located. Over one-third of its food supply is the subterranean fungus Endogone, which this mouse probably finds using its keen sense of smell. Science knows little about Endogone because it is difficult for people to find.

BIRDS

Sharp-shinned Hawk, Cooper's Hawk (not illustrated), Northern Goshawk

These Accipiters (bird eaters) are similar in appearance and occupy the same habitat. Size is the best clue to identification, but it takes some experience to judge relative size when the birds are not seen together. After seeing each bird a few times, you will see that the Northern Goshawk is the largest, the Cooper's Hawk is intermediate in size, and the Sharp-shinned Hawk is the smallest of the three. Look for stick nests in winter high in a crotch of a hardwood tree, and watch from a distance for these Tug Hill breeders to return in spring. Active nests will be decorated with fresh twigs, usually softwood, when they are being prepared for nesting in early spring. All three of these hawks are wary and quick to take flight, even when observed on a kill.

Great Horned Owl

The Great Horned Owl is a year 'round resident that may lay its eggs as early as January, often in old hawk nests. Occupation of a nest by owls is unmistakable, by April the ground will be littered with various cast-off parts of prey and pellets. The 'horns' are actually ear tufts. Incubation is done by both sexes and both adults feed the young. Feeding continues on the ground after the young leave the nest but before they are able to fly well. The Great Horned Owl seems to relish Skunk, and it is apparently not bothered by the odor.

Eastern Screech-Owl

This owl occurs in a red and a gray *morph* (variation in plumage color that is unrelated to sex or season). The gray morph is more common on the Hill. Listen for the mournful whinny or wail at night in spring when the birds are mating, and in the fall when they are moving to winter habitat. Birders imitate the call to attract other birds that will gather to mob the owl as a predatory threat. Adults have been known to attack people near a nest tree and even strike them to drive them away. This owl feeds on small mammals and small birds.

Pileated Woodpecker

The Pileated Woodpecker cuts long oval holes in dead trees, searching for Carpenter Ants, its preferred food. This bird also works on stumps and rotten logs looking for the grubs of wood boring beetles. Watch for this large crow-sized bird, flying from trunk to trunk with slow, full wingbeats. Listen for its heavy, descending drumming sound and loud, prehistoric-sounding cry, *'yucka-yucka-yucka'*.

Chimney Swift

This neotropical migrant is a very fast flyer, feeding on the wing on large numbers of flying insects. Listen for a twittering overhead as a group of Chimney Swifts dives and swoops for insect prey. The bird's cigar-shaped body is small in relation to its wing area and, since it seldom lands, its feet are small and weak. Nesting materials are snatched from treetops in flight, and the nest is placed on the inside wall of a chimney or tree cavity with a sticky saliva material.

Great Crested Flycatcher

The call of this neotropical migrant, a loud whistled 'wheep'or a rolling 'prrree', will send you searching the treetops for a look at the caller.

Brown Creeper

The Brown Creeper was named for its habit of creeping around the trunks and limbs of trees, searching for insects under the bark. Sit still and listen for high, single peeps and scratching sounds from the trunks of trees. This bird can be seen at any season of the year.

Wood Thrush, Hermit Thrush (not illustrated), Swainson's Thrush (not illustrated)

These birds are similar in appearance and they are all neotropical migrants whose populations have dwindled in recent years. All three are very shy, but they are commonly heard singing in the deep woods at dusk and dawn. Their songs are serene and melancholy, a series of clear flute like notes, the similar phrases repeated at different pitches. It takes study to distinguish one song from the other. Look for the birds on a low branch or sapling, or picking through the leaf litter in the understory of dark woods.

Red-eyed Vireo

The common Red-eyed Vireo is a neotropical migrant. It is difficult to see its red eye without good binoculars, since the bird rarely leaves the hardwood canopy. This bird is most easily found in spring before the leaves fully break out of bud. This vireo's song is an almost continuous 'hear me, see me, here i am, over here'.

Scarlet Tanager

The Scarlet Tanager, a neotropical migrant, returns from its winter range in May and starts singing from treetops early in the morning. This bird's song is robin-like but more hoarse. Look for the bird in the heart of a mature forest patch.

REPTILES

Red-bellied Snake

The Red-bellied Snake is a small, secretive, and harmless serpent that spends most of its time under rocks and logs throughout forested parts of Tug Hill. This snake gives birth to live young that are 3 inches long and no bigger around than a toothpick. Red-bellied Snakes feed on slugs, worms, and soft-bodied insects.

INSECTS

Cecropia Moth (Robin Moth) (not illustrated)

The Cecropia is the largest North American moth. Look for it along with many other woodland moths in the daytime on a tree or wall, near a nightlight, or around your lantern at night. The large larva (up to 4 3/8 inches) winters in a cocoon that it constructs and attaches lengthwise along a twig. It feeds on many trees and shrubs including apple, ash, beech, elm, maple, poplar, cherry, and willow. Look for the cocoon at the woodland edges and in shrublands on winter walks.

Eastern Tent Caterpillar, Forest Tent Caterpillar (not illustrated)

This insect is best known to us in its larval form and is easy to find. The Forest Tent Caterpillar does not make the tent-like webbing made by the Eastern Tent Caterpillar, but may defoliate large forest tracts of hardwood trees such as maple, cherry, poplar, aspen, and willow. These outbreaks tend to be cyclic and crash after a few years as parasites and disease take their toll on the high population of caterpillars that develop. Heavy populations of the Eastern Tent Caterpillar are evident when all the cherry trees are denuded in late summer and covered with webs. In heavy infestations, the adult moths will be seen flying at all hours of the day and night.

Luna Moth

The easiest place to find a Luna Moth is at a light near a forested area. Look for one resting in the morning on a pole or building with a nightlight. The larvae feed on many species of trees such as alder, beech, cherry, hazelnut, hickory, and willow. The cocoon is concealed on the ground in leaf litter over the winter.

Snow Flea

The Snow Flea is a tiny, wingless insect that occurs by the thousands in each square foot of the forest floor, and is a very important decomposer in the food chain. Each gray individual is so small it is hard to see, but when thousands congregate on the snow surface, the group is easy to observe. Sometimes you can find a mass of fleas on the trunk of a tree in spring. The Snow Flea cannot fly, but it propels itself into the air by releasing a tiny prong from a hook on its underside that pushes against the ground with great force.

Sow Bug (not illustrated)

The Sow Bug belongs to the only group of Crustaceans (crabs, lobsters, crayfish, etc.) that has successfully invaded the land. They are called Isopods and are gill-breathers, so they require a moist habitat. Lift up any decaying log and you will find them in the damp places below (be sure to put the log back the way you found it). Use a flashlight at night to look for a Sow Bug crawling around on the surface, feeding on decaying vegetation under the cover of darkness. Another Isopod, the Pillbug, rolls into a ball when disturbed.

Millepedes

The Millepede is another occupant of rotting logs. Two very large forms, one black and cylindrical with small segments and one flattened with large segments, may be found on Tug Hill. The black Millepede rolls into a spiral coil if you dare to pick it up. Each segment of the Millepede's body has two pair of legs. The Millepede feeds on decomposing plant material and is important in returning nutrients to the soil.

Centipedes

The Centipede, like the Millepede, is made up of many repeated segments. Each segment behind the head possesses a single pair of legs. It also has a pair of pincer-like claws near its head that are capable of delivering a powerful poison to its prey. Most species are bright red in color, a warning to would-be predators that they should not be disturbed. None of the species of Centipedes that occur on the Hill are dangerous to people, though their bites can be painful.

Photo by Robert McNamara

MIXED HARDWOODS
AND SOFTWOODS
VERIFYING CHARACTERISTICS

- Scattered Hemlocks and Pines among Hardwoods
- Young Hemlocks in Understory
- Pits and Mounds on Forest Floor
- Dense Stands of Evergreens in Lower Areas, and on Ridges

"My son, your son, they aren't going to have a (forest) resource as we know it unless we use it right"

Tim Engst

From a high vantage point you can see that the hardwood forest is decorated in many places with scattered softwood trees and edged, or lined, with dense stands of softwoods. Individual white pines penetrate the hardwood canopy. Stands of softwoods may border marshes and wet meadows in localized habitats. These small patches of mixed hardwoods and softwoods can be found throughout the region, but there are two places where the softwoods comprise a major part of the habitat. If you study a satellite photo, you will see these places as dark green patches that dominate the landscape. One place, located in the southwestern corner of the region, is the Oneida Lake Forest. The soils, groundwater, and subtle climatic differences in the area between NYS Routes 13 and 49 favor white pine and hemlock in higher concentrations than in other parts of the region. The second place is the northeastern flank of the core forest where crescent shaped stands of Red Spruce and Balsam Fir occupy the highest elevations.

Go find one of the **Eastern White Pines** that you saw towering above the canopy and stand at its base. The first Europeans on the Continent probably did the same thing. Early explorers saw ship masts in these primeval giants. If you are lucky you may find a tree that comes close to the majesty that impressed the explorers. Some giants still stand tall and straight, 4 feet in diameter, 50-60 feet to the first branch, and

51

with deeply furrowed bark. You are most likely to find these large trees on a remote slope or on an elevated island in a wet area. In second and third growth forests the *terminal* (topmost) shoot of the pines is killed by a boring insect called the White Pine Weevil. The weevil drills a hole in the stem and deposits eggs. The loss of the main leader causes side shoots to develop faster, much like pruning a shrub, and the tree bushes out into a form foresters call a *wolf tree*. Listen closely, near a recently fallen limb or dead tree, for a repetitious crunching sound. You can hear the larvae of the **Pine Sawyer** chewing its way out of the chamber where it was deposited as an egg. A dead white pine on the forest floor hosts a menagerie of insect life. Centipedes, millipedes, sowbugs, and beetles quickly invade it, and its nutrients are returned to the soil.

Look for owl pellets on the forest floor around the tree. Owls often roost in the white pines and regurgitate the inedible portions of their meals of whole rodents and birds in the form of hairy, papery clumps called *pellets*. Break a pellet apart and you will find the bones of the owl's prey. Sometimes you can find an owl spending the day on a white pine limb very close to the trunk. The camouflaged coloration of owls makes them very difficult to spot.

Look under almost any rotting log and you will find a **Red-backed Salamander**. It is the most numerous *vertebrate* (having a backbone) animal in the forest. Despite their small size, if you could weigh all of

Red-backed Salamander

the Red-backed Salamanders in a given area of forest, they would weigh more than all the deer that inhabit that same area. This fact emphasizes the ecological importance of this tiny amphibian in the flow of energy from one food web to another. Salamanders are the lions and tigers of the decomposing food web. They are a major part of the diet of birds, snakes, and mammals, and they repackage energy into a form that would otherwise be unavailable to these larger predators.

Spring

Listen for high-pitched peeping calls from pines and hemlocks and watch for flashes of color from the hyperactive feeding of kinglets and warblers. Two different kinglets and as many as 25 different warbler species migrate across the Hill in the spring and fall. Many of the species nest on the Hill. The tiny birds you see in May are on an annual journey from Central and South America to nesting sites in the north. Birds that make this flight are called *neotropical migrants*. Spring is the best time to see these butterflies of the bird world since it is the time when they are in bright breeding plumage. You will need to be quick with your binoculars and keep the sun at your back to see these tiny but brilliant songbirds. The **Black-throated Green Warbler** sings a characteristic song as it flits through the canopy feeding on beetles, flies, moths, foliage-eating caterpillars, cankerworms, and leafrollers. Listen for four high-pitched, wheezy notes followed by one lower and one higher, *'zee zee zee zee zoo zee'*. If it is May and you are in the mixed forest you will hear these notes.

You may think that your solitude is being broken by the sound of an engine trying to start. At a regular interval, the engine fires up, increases in speed, then sputters out. The sound is actually made by a male **Ruffed Grouse**, commonly called a *Partridge*, advertising for a mate. The grouse digs its toenails into a rotting log and beats its wings against its breast to make the noise. You can find a drumming log by looking for a pile of droppings near a stump or log in an area where you have heard the sound. Examine the stump or log for scratch marks or shredded wood fibers to identify the drumming spot.

Summer

You may need insect repellent and a headnet to explore the mixed forest in early summer. The moist air and shelter are perfect for biting insects. Many people despise and even curse insects, but they are an important link in energy flow in the forest ecosystem. The many forms and habits of insects are fascinating if you can overcome your dread. If you are in an area with sandy soils, look under a recent windthrow or clearing for perfect funnel-shaped depressions in the sand. Watch closely and you will see movement beneath the sand at the bottom of the funnel. The funnel is a clever trap made by the larva of an **Antlion**. If an ant, or any insect, wanders into the funnel it will have trouble climbing up the loose sand slope. To make matters worse, the Antlion senses the presence of a victim and throws more sand at it. When the insect slips to within reach, large pincer-like jaws come out of the sand, grab the victim, and drag it under. The Antlion then sucks the juices from the insect and kicks the dry carcass out of the hole. These louse-like larvae metamorphose into large, lacy-winged flying insects that do not live in sand and have no pincers.

A bird that is easy to hear but hard to see is the **Ovenbird**. It spends almost all of its time on the forest floor and is well camouflaged. It announces its presence with a loud, sharp, *'teacher Teacher TEACHER'*. The Ovenbird builds a domed nest of leaves on the ground that looks somewhat like an earthen oven, hence its name. The nest blends so perfectly with the forest floor it is nearly impossible to find.

Fall

An eerie screaming from under the hemlocks could be the sound of a female **Porcupine**. The Porcupine mates on the ground. After the male has liberally sprayed the female with urine she arches her back so that he is not stuck with quills, and he mounts her from the rear. When copulation is over, the female screams at the male and drives him away. The Porcupine usually gives birth to only one pup in a den in rocks, brush piles, abandoned buildings, or hollow trees. The den is easy to find, it is usually marked by a large mound of droppings at the entrance. People are the most ruthless predator of the Porcupine. The *herbivorous* (plant eating) animal is persecuted for grazing hemlocks and other trees, but people in Porcupine territory know it for gnawing on anything rubber; car tires, hoses, and wire insulation. A Porcupine will even chew up the seat of an outhouse. This odd behavior is caused by a need for small quantities of certain minerals that the animal does not get from its normal vegetable fare. Look for fresh clippings littering the ground around a hemlock and you may find a Porcupine in the treetop. The shiny white tree trunks and limbs you sometimes see on beeches and aspens are the result of winter

Porcupine

feeding on the cambium layer of the bark. This starvation diet is not the preferred fare of the Porcupine. Most of the year the Porcupine eats herbaceous vegetation; dandelion, clover, water-lily, and Skunk Cabbage.

The Great Horned Owl, coyote, bobcat, and bear will eat a Porcupine, but the celebrated natural predator is the **Fisher**. The Fisher, a native species that had been *extirpated* (eliminated from a portion of its natural range) has been re-introduced to many areas of North America to help re-establish natural Porcupine control. The Fisher faces the Porcupine and attacks its nose and face with lightning speed. When it has killed the Porcupine the Fisher flips the victim over and eats through the unprotected body.

Winter

Give a hoot at dusk and you may be answered by a **Barred Owl**. Go into the woods on a moonlit winter night and listen for a deep, resonant hoot or try to coax an owl into responding to an imitation of its call. The call of this owl is a series of 8 hoots ending in *'oo-aw'*, and it is said to sound like *'who cooks for you? who cooks for you-all?'* The imitation does not have to be very good to get a response if you are in an owl's territory. The bird is a year 'round resident and calls in all seasons, any time of day or night. During the day listen for an excited gathering of crows and you may be able to follow them to the roosting owl that they are *mobbing* (crowding around and calling excitedly). Crows and other birds mob owls and hawks to overwhelm them and drive them away. The Barred Owl nests as early as February in a tree cavity or old hawk nest.

Red-breasted Nuthatch

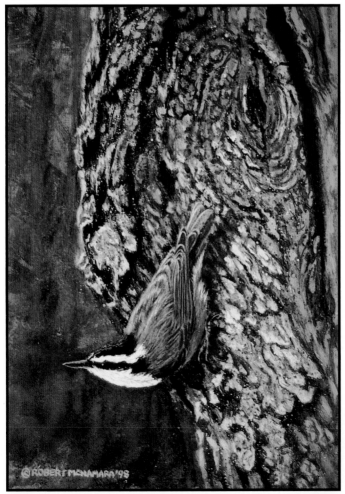

Painting by Robert McNamara

ILLUSTRATIONS

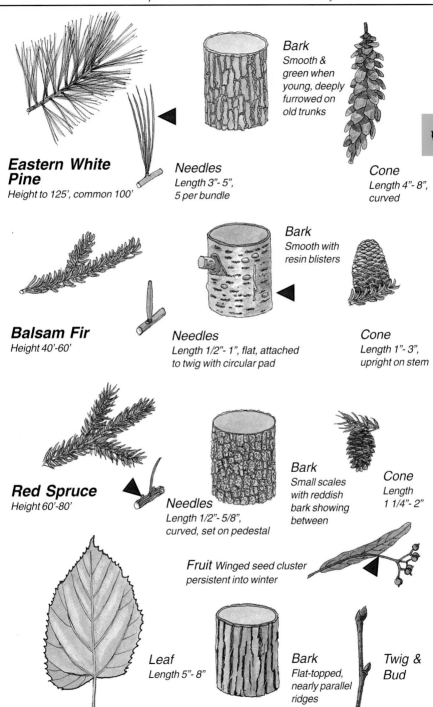

Eastern White Pine
Height to 125', common 100'

Bark
Smooth & green when young, deeply furrowed on old trunks

Needles
Length 3"- 5", 5 per bundle

Cone
Length 4"- 8", curved

Balsam Fir
Height 40'-60'

Bark
Smooth with resin blisters

Needles
Length 1/2"- 1", flat, attached to twig with circular pad

Cone
Length 1"- 3", upright on stem

Red Spruce
Height 60'-80'

Bark
Small scales with reddish bark showing between

Needles
Length 1/2"- 5/8", curved, set on pedestal

Cone
Length 1 1/4"- 2"

Fruit *Winged seed cluster persistent into winter*

Leaf
Length 5"- 8"

Bark
Flat-topped, nearly parallel ridges

Twig & Bud

American Basswood
Height to 125', common 50'-80'

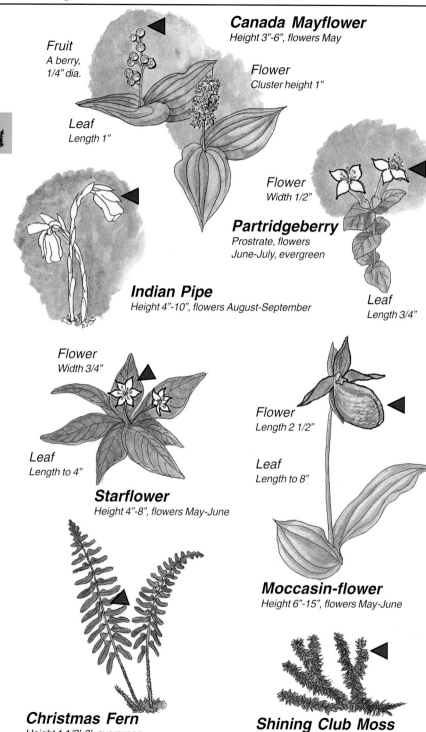

Canada Mayflower
Height 3"-6", flowers May

Fruit
A berry,
1/4" dia.

Flower
Cluster height 1"

Leaf
Length 1"

Flower
Width 1/2"

Partridgeberry
Prostrate, flowers
June-July, evergreen

Indian Pipe
Height 4"-10", flowers August-September

Leaf
Length 3/4"

Flower
Width 3/4"

Flower
Length 2 1/2"

Leaf
Length to 4"

Leaf
Length to 8"

Starflower
Height 4"-8", flowers May-June

Moccasin-flower
Height 6"-15", flowers May-June

Christmas Fern
Height 1 1/2'-2', evergreen

Shining Club Moss
Height 6", evergreen

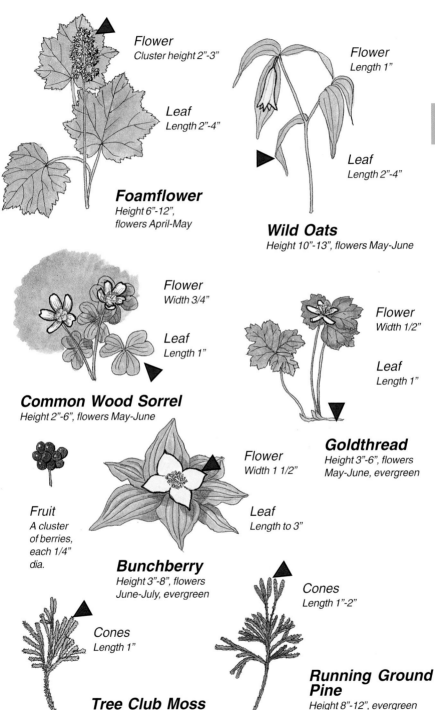

Flower
Cluster height 2"-3"

Leaf
Length 2"-4"

Foamflower
Height 6"-12",
flowers April-May

Flower
Length 1"

Leaf
Length 2"-4"

Wild Oats
Height 10"-13", flowers May-June

Flower
Width 3/4"

Leaf
Length 1"

Common Wood Sorrel
Height 2"-6", flowers May-June

Flower
Width 1/2"

Leaf
Length 1"

Goldthread
Height 3"-6", flowers
May-June, evergreen

Fruit
A cluster
of berries,
each 1/4"
dia.

Flower
Width 1 1/2"

Leaf
Length to 3"

Bunchberry
Height 3"-8", flowers
June-July, evergreen

Cones
Length 1"

Tree Club Moss
Height 8"-12", evergreen

Cones
Length 1"-2"

Running Ground Pine
Height 8"-12", evergreen

Yellow-bellied Sapsucker
Length 8"
Look for fresh rows
of holes in tree trunk

**Northern
Goshawk**
Length 24"
Wingspan 42"
Alternately flaps
& sails in flight,
rarely soars

Northern Saw-whet Owl
Length 8"
Wingspan 18"
Daytime roosts in evergreens on limb
close to trunk

Barred Owl
Length 20"
Wingspan 44"
Dark eyes, barred
breast, call often
heard in daytime

**Ruffed
Grouse**
Length 16"
Wingspan 24"
When one bird is
flushed, study the
undergrowth for others

Rose-breasted Grosbeak
Length 8"
Song like Robin, call a loud 'peek'

Black-throated Green Warbler
Length 5"
Very active in treetops

Ruby-crowned Kinglet
Length 4 1/2"
Feeds in the middle of evergreen trees

Golden-crowned Kinglet
Length 4"
Call a series of very high-pitched notes in threes

White-breasted Nuthatch
Length 5 3/4"
Call a nasal 'yank yank yank'

Red-breasted Nuthatch
Length 4 1/2"
Feeds upside down on tree trunk

White-throated Sparrow
Length 6 3/4"
Feeds on forest floor

Ovenbird
Length 6"
Feeds on forest floor

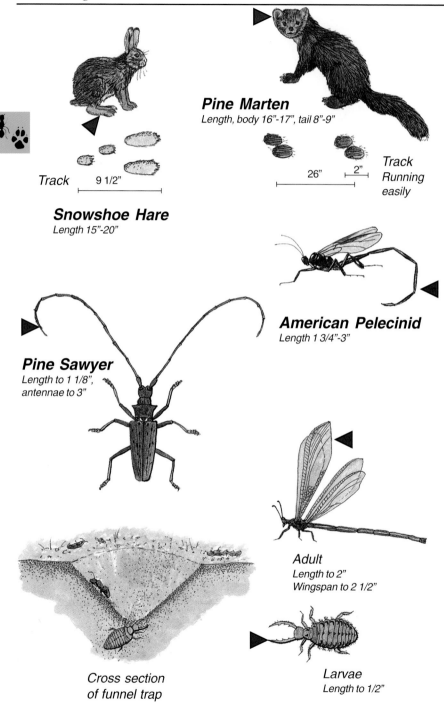

Pine Marten
Length, body 16"-17", tail 8"-9"

Track

Track   9 1/2"

26"   2"

Track
*Running
easily*

Snowshoe Hare
Length 15"-20"

American Pelecinid
Length 1 3/4"-3"

Pine Sawyer
*Length to 1 1/8",
antennae to 3"*

Adult
*Length to 2"
Wingspan to 2 1/2"*

*Cross section
of funnel trap*

Larvae
Length to 1/2"

Antlion

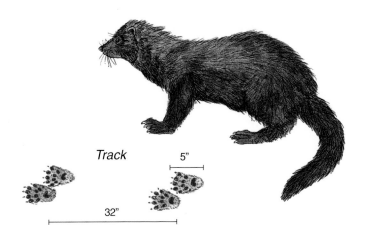

Track

5"

32"

Fisher
Length, body 20"-25", tail 13"-15"

FACTS, TIPS, AND LORE

FACTS, TIPS, AND LORE
MIXED HARDWOODS
AND SOFTWOODS

TREES

Eastern White Pine

The Eastern White Pine is the tallest Tug Hill tree and one of the most common softwoods; look for isolated individuals towering above the canopy. Upper limbs of this tree survive better on the leeward side, resulting in a *'flagged'* form, an indicator of prevailing wind direction. This pine is a very fast growing tree and its wood is light, soft, and relatively weak.

Red Spruce

This softwood member of the transitional forest is a representative of northern plant communities, consequently it is most abundant on the highest elevations. The wood is used for sounding boards in musical instruments. The new growth needles can be mixed with molasses or honey and fermented to make spruce beer. At one time spruce gum was a valuable product, used as a base for chewing gum. Some Tug Hill residents once wandered far and wide on spruce gum forays.

Balsam Fir

Balsam Fir is a companion of Red Spruce in northern plant communities, and it is also most abundant at higher elevations, usually in wet situations. This tree is sometimes found in pastures, where it is avoided by the cows because of its distasteful resin. This resin, the source of the very pleasant fragrance of the balsam, is used for microscopic slides because of its optical clarity. Many products use balsam, from pillows to nasal decongestant. Balsam is a favorite Christmas tree since it holds its needles and it is so fragrant.

SHRUBS

Hobblebush

Hobblebush is a leggy shrub named for the tangle of stems that make walking through it difficult. Stems exhibit *adventitious rooting* (they root wherever they touch the ground). The showy flowers of this plant bloom very early in spring and look somewhat like Flowering Dogwood. The large leaves of the shrub color bronze in the fall. The tan buds of Hobblebush are *naked* (they are not enclosed by bud scales) and look like clasped hands.

HERBACEOUS PLANTS

Goldthread

This low-growing plant with three-parted evergreen leaves can be found in moist areas of the mixed forest and in conifer swamps. It is named for the golden color of its threadlike roots. The roots contain berberidine, which is the source of the brownish-yellow antiseptic cleansing agent used prior to surgery. Native Americans and settlers made a bitter brew from the roots for sore throats and ulcerated mouths. Fungus gnats and fungus-feeding beetles are the primary pollinators; look for a gnat in the flower on sunny June days.

Moccasin-flower (Pink Ladyslipper)

The Moccasin-flower does not self-pollinate, but is most often fertilized by bees. Bees can enter the flower fairly easily to feast on nectar, but the passage out is narrow. The bee must pass over sticky hairs which comb pollen from another flower off the bee, then on its way out the bee brushes against new pollen. Sometimes bees bite their way out, or even die within the flower. Moccasin-flowers and other orchids have a *symbiotic* (both rely on each other) relationship with fungi and will not survive if transplanted from their native habitat.

Common Wood Sorrel

This plant grows in rich damp woods. The shamrock-shaped leaves close at night, and have a slightly sour taste, somewhat like diluted vinegar. It is usually associated with hemlocks and damp soils.

Indian Pipe

Indian Pipe is white because it does not contain chlorophyll for *photosynthesis* (the process that green plants use to convert sunlight to energy). It is a *saprophyte* (it gets its nutrients from decaying plant material). After flowering, the single nodding flower becomes an erect fruit capsule and the whole plant turns brown.

MOSSES

Clubmoss, Ground Cedar, Running Ground Pine

These common components of Christmas wreaths and garlands look like miniature pines or cedars. They are not related to trees, nor are they a moss; they are actually closely related to ferns and are referred to as *fern allies*. They have descended from an ancient plant family that was part of the fern tree jungles of the Paleozoic Era, 300 million years ago. The spores by which they reproduce have been used for many commercial purposes. Since the spores burn explosively, they were used as the flash for early photography, and because of their powder-like quality they were used to coat pills to prevent them from sticking together.

Common Hairy Cap Moss (not illustrated)

This moss forms bed-like patches that invite you to lie on them.

Pin Cushion Moss (not illustrated)

Pin Cushion Moss is green when wet, but has a whitish cast when dry. This moss grows in little pin cushion-like mounds and can spread when mounds become detached from their growing surface, roll or blow away, and then re-attach themselves in a new location.

MAMMALS

Deer Mouse

The Deer Mouse is nocturnal, which is indicated by its large black eyes, and it may scritch and scratch all night long around lean-tos or camps. This mouse is a very good climber, and it often sleeps or rests in squirrel nests or cavities high above ground. The Deer Mouse track looks like a miniature rabbit track in fresh snow because it moves in a series of leaps, except the tail leaves a visible mark. Seeds and nuts of forest plants, seed heads of grasses in clearings, berries, and insects are cached to supply food for winter, since this mouse does not hibernate.

Red Squirrel

Most of us have been scolded by a bold Red Squirrel. This squirrel is also responsible for the bombarding pinecones that seem to come out of the canopy at an astonishing rate. The caches of cones are used year after year and the piles of cone pieces can get large. The Red Squirrel also eats mushrooms, even those poisonous to people.

Porcupine

The Porcupine is a large native rodent, second in size only to the Beaver, the largest of the North American rodents. The Porcupine's quills are modified hairs and all the hairs on the back can be raised when the animal is alarmed. A Porcupine in defensive mode will lower its head and shoulders, raise its heavily muscled tail, and prepare to quickly spin around and drive its thick tail quills into the attacker. Contrary to old tales, a Porcupine can not throw its quills. The sharp end of each quill is usually dark in color, and is covered with small hooks, or barbs. When a quill is embedded in the attacker's tissue, it expands, and, as the attacker's muscles contract, the quill is pulled farther into the tissue. These quills can prove fatal to many attackers, although the Porcupines themselves are dexterous enough to remove them with their incisors and forefeet.

Fisher

The Fisher, the largest member of the weasel family in New York, is now a common sight on the Hill. Look for the characteristic weasel track pattern of two slightly offset prints repeated at an even interval, with footprints as big as those of a medium-sized dog. Follow the tracks and you may find a Fisher den in a large hollow tree. The Fisher is an excellent climber and quick enough to catch a Red Squirrel. Since winter-killed deer are an important food source, hide near a carcass to catch site of a Fisher.

Pine Marten

The Pine Marten is rare on the Hill because it requires dense cover and avoids open areas and forests where logging has occurred. This member of the weasel family is famous for its ability to chase Red Squirrels through the treetops and overtake them. In the winter Pine Martens hunt for rodents beneath the snow by tunneling under fallen logs and stumps. They den in a tree cavity well off the ground. Leaving den trees behind when logging is important in maintaining shelter for this and many other mammals and birds.

Bobcat

The Bobcat is wary and difficult to see, but it is fairly common on the Hill. It is most often seen from a deer stand or by watching a winter-killed carcass. Although finding this cat's tracks in winter may be the closest you will get, it is still a thrill. A Bobcat appears large because of its long legs and thick fur, but most cats weigh only 15-30 pounds. Bobcat dens in hollow trees or stumps can be confirmed by the cat-like odor around them.

BIRDS

Ruffed Grouse (Partridge)

Startling when flushed from cover, the Ruffed Grouse is a favorite game bird. Two color phases of this bird occur in New York State: the dark phase, the most common, and the red phase, found in open habitats. The Ruffed Grouse is a year 'round resident that makes snow beds in deep snow by plunging and burrowing beneath the powder, and it is often seen feeding on aspen buds on a late winter day. A young grouse is *precocial* (it is born ready to travel) and is capable of flying short distances to escape predators, even when its feathers are still in the down stage. The Ruffed Grouse is nicknamed *Foolbird* because of its occasional strange behavior. These birds have been known to follow people who enter their territory and peck at their feet. Ruffed Grouse make a variety of noises and pretend to be injured when an animal or a person approaches their nest in an attempt to lure it away.

Northern Goshawk

The Northern Goshawk is the largest of the Accipiters found in New York. Like all birds of prey, the male is smaller than the female. The bird is often seen as it rapidly crosses an open road or flies out of a hemlock stand where it has been hunting for Ruffed Grouse, its favorite prey species. The Goshawk has been known to attack people who approach a nest and inflict wounds to the back and head. People and Great Horned Owls are this bird's major enemies. A Great Horned Owl will seek out and kill a female Goshawk attempting to nest in its territory.

Black-throated Green Warbler

This neotropical migrant breeds and nests on Tug Hill in softwoods and mixed forests. The nest is a small cup of grass, moss, plant fibers, and spider webs lined with a thick felting of hair, fur, rootlets, and feathers.

White-throated Sparrow

This bird is more often heard than seen as it sits atop a conifer tree and sings its plaintive song, a clear, whistled, '*sweet sweet Canada, Canada, Canada*'. The song is associated with a wild mountain setting and the bird is most likely to be spotted in the higher elevations of the Hill. This sparrow nests on the ground in softwood cover and can often be heard scratching in the leaves for seeds and insects.

Rose-breasted Grosbeak

The Rose-breasted Grosbeak, unlike its more conspicuous relative the Evening Grosbeak, is a neotropical migrant. This grosbeak spends its summer on Tug Hill, while the Evening Grosbeak is a winter visitor. The male bird will often sit on the nest and sing a robin-like song while the female is away feeding.

Ruby-crowned Kinglet, Golden-crowned Kinglet

The Ruby-crowned Kinglet is one of two kinglets found on the Hill; the other is the Golden-crowned Kinglet. The crown of the Ruby-crowned Kinglet is indistinct until flashed by an irritated bird. Both birds can be seen during migration moving through the softwood trees. Listen for a series of thin '*tsee*' notes repeated frequently from within the boughs of a softwood, and watch for the quick movements of the tiny bird.

Red-breasted Nuthatch

The Red-breasted Nuthatch breeds on Tug Hill and is a year 'round resident. This nuthatch is more closely associated with softwood trees than the White-breasted Nuthatch. Look for this bird working over cones to get at the seeds. In years of low cone production many birds temporarily leave the Hill and move south where food sources are more plentiful.

White-breasted Nuthatch

The White-breasted Nuthatch is commonly seen working a hardwood tree at every level, searching under bark and at branch joints for insects and spiders. The bird nests in a hollow stump or branch.

Yellow-bellied Sapsucker

This woodpecker is responsible for the horizontal lines of small holes in the bark of apple and other hardwood trees, and in some softwoods like Red Spruce. The holes are drilled through the bark to start the tree sap flowing. The bird later returns to the tree to eat the sap and the insects that it has attracted and trapped. You can find trees that have been tapped over many years.

Northern Saw-whet Owl

The Northern Saw-whet Owl is the smallest owl breeding on the Hill, and the least known. The bird is only active at night, and spends the day hidden in a dense softwood tree. Listen for chickadees, nuthatches, and other birds chattering excitedly in a group, as they may be mobbing a saw-whet. The bird is tame when found, allowing close approach. The call of the saw-whet is a mellow, whistled note repeated mechanically in long succession, often between 100 and 130 times per minute. At a distance the call has a bell like quality that those who named the bird likened to the sound of a saw blade played as a musical instrument in a jug band.

AMPHIBIANS

Red-backed Salamander

A Red-backed Salamander breathes through its skin and can not leave moist places. During dry spells it moves deeper into the leaf litter. This salamander lays eggs on land. Metamorphosis from the larva to the adult occurs directly in the egg, freeing the salamander from the aquatic existence that other amphibians require.

INSECTS

Pine Sawyer

The adult Pine Sawyer is also known as the *Long-horned Beetle* because of its impressive antennae. The female deposits eggs under the bark of the tree, and when they hatch, the larva feed on the *heartwood* (the non-growing wood that makes up most of the tree trunk) and *sapwood* (the growing layer of wood just beneath the bark) of the tree until they *pupate* (make a cocoon). When the adult emerges from the cocoon, it chews its way out of the tree.

Woodland Accent - Magnolia Warbler and Hobblebush

SUCCESSIONAL FORESTS

VERIFYING CHARACTERISTICS

- Scattered Gray Birch, or Aspen Trees
- Abundant Understory Growth
- Understory Tree Species Different from Canopy Species

*" The forest can still be used commercially
but it should be preserved as a heritage
for all future generations"*

John Constable, Jr.

What is it if it is neither hardwood forest nor pasture? It is a variable plant community that is in transition from field to forest. This process is called *plant succession*. A forest that is disturbed by fire, blowdown, insect infestation, or the activities of people will tend to regenerate to its former mature state. If you see Gray Birch or Quaking Aspen trees you are most likely looking at a successional forest. **Gray Birch** is sometimes called *White* or *Paper Birch*, but the true Paper Birch is a prominent member of the high elevation Adirondack forest. Gray Birch, the most common white-barked birch found on the Hill, is a *pioneer species*, a plant that invades open areas after a disturbance like fire or logging, and is eventually replaced by more shade-tolerant species as the forest grows more dense and the canopy closes.

Successional forests in various stages of transition cover large areas of the Hill. The abandonment of the 19th century subsistence farms and continued logging keeps the forest in early stages of succession. The more extensive the openings in the canopy, the earlier a stage of re-vegetation will result. The variations in age classes of the successional forest on the Hill are great, due to different intensities of harvesting and different times of farm abandonment. Consequently, there is a tremendous diversity of habitat and species. Though the successional forests of the Tug Hill are varied, they all share a common element;

they are composed of an irregular canopy of medium-sized trees consisting mainly of pioneer species such as Gray Birch, Quaking Aspen, and Balsam Fir.

Spring

What is the tree that blooms with white flowers before any other buds have opened? It is called the **Serviceberry,** or *Shadbush*, because it blooms at the same time that the *shad* (a small migratory fish) moves upstream to spawn in some rivers. The showy, flowering tree signals the arrival of warm weather with its blossoms and can be found in the openings and along the edges of the forest. The bloom is not the only attraction; its sweet purple fruit matures in June, but you will be lucky to find any before the birds get them. Both a tree-like and a multi-stemmed variety have a pleasing shape when open-grown, making Serviceberry a great ornamental plant.

Listen for a loud trilling call starting at dusk and lasting through the night. You may wonder what bird sings at night, but the call is actually coming from a treefrog. The **Gray Treefrog** is the only true treefrog on

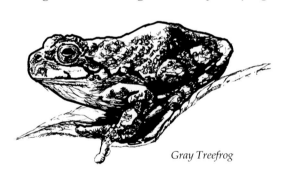

Tug Hill. Calling sites are usually in the lower branches of trees. This treefrog has *'suction cup'* toe pads that help it climb. The adult is mostly gray with black splotches, but it can change its color pattern and may appear bright green to silvery.

Gray Treefrog

The most visible beneficiaries of the diversity of habitat in the successional forest are songbirds. Spring is the best time to see the colorful migrants as they take advantage of abundant insects. Walk along forest edges and watch for the small but colorful **Magnolia Warbler** flitting from branch to branch, feeding on insects. Study the tree tops for similar feeding activities and you could spot the yellow-orange flash of a **Blackburnian Warbler**.

Summer

Scan the ground as you walk along on a bright sunny day and watch for a shiny insect darting ahead of you as you approach, just far enough so you cannot get a good look at it. If you are patient and move very slowly, you may see a tiger beetle. This small beetle is well named because it is a major predator, both as an adult and as a larva. A tiger beetle is marvelously adapted for eating other insects. It has a pair of powerful pincers around its mouth and long delicate legs that allow it to speed over the bare ground it prefers for hunting. The *Six-spotted Green Tiger Beetle* has a brilliantly iridescent green shell with six white spots.

Listen at night for a well-known repetitious sound from forest openings. The song of the *Whip-poor-will* is more complex when heard close-up. Sneak toward the sound at dusk and you may get a look at the caller lying flat on a rock or sandy spot. The eyes of the bird reflect a beam of light with a red glow. During the day the bird lies flat and parallel on a tree branch, its camouflage coloration making it look almost like a part of the tree. When the song is sung all night outside a bedroom window it has been known to try the patience of many a sleepy Tug Hill resident.

Fall

In September and October, the steady 3-note chirping calls of the *Snowy Tree Cricket* are a dominant feature of Tug Hill evenings. The interval between chirps is temperature dependent. The change in the interval is so regular that you can count the number of chirps in 14 seconds, add 40, and obtain a reasonable estimate of the temperature in degrees Fahrenheit. The male produces this sound from its shrub or tree perch to attract a female for the purpose of mating. As with other crickets, the edges of the left and right wing covers are rubbed across each other to produce the sound.

The *Quaking Aspen*, or *Popple*, is one of the most conspicuous trees of the successional forest, especially in the fall, when the leaves turn a brilliant yellow-gold. Aspen stands can show an almost even gradation in height from the center toward the edges as the *suckers* (tree shoots that sprout from the underground parts of older trees) invade an open space. The spreading mass of suckers can be centuries old, having spread along its edges as the older sections were replaced by climax species.

Winter

Would you look in a tree to see a canine? If you were looking for a *Gray Fox*, you could find one in a .tree. When chased by enemies, it will climb the trunk of a tree like a bear, or jump, cat-like, from branch to branch to safety. Northern New York is the northern limit of the range of the Gray Fox. It is the size of a small dog, and can be distinguished from the Red Fox most easily by the black tip on its tail. The Gray Fox prefers the diversity of successional forests with nearby open areas because these areas often have high rodent populations. A fox track is not much bigger than a cat track, but, unlike a cat track, a clear fox track should show claw marks. The tracks will wander for miles. If you have the stamina you may find, in a hollow tree or hole in a bank or knoll, one of the many dens a fox will use. Follow a fresh fox track and you will be able to visualize the early morning feeding activity, as the fox searches from brush pile to grass clump for rabbits and other rodents. The Gray Fox will also eat weasels, skunks, owls, hawks, raccoons, snakes, and even trout. Look for evidence of a catch; fur, feathers, or a drop of blood left behind in the snow.

Look in the snow for tracks and tunnels of the small animals the fox is seeking. All of those mouse-like animals are not mice. In addition to the Deer, Jumping, and White-footed Mouse, there are several species of voles and moles. The reproduction rate of some small mammals is legendary. Theoretical calculations show that an initial population of 1600 voles per square mile could reproduce to create a density of 142,400 voles per square mile in one summer. This prolific reproduction makes small animals a critical part of the food chain, and reminds us of the important role of predators in controlling their populations.

ILLUSTRATIONS

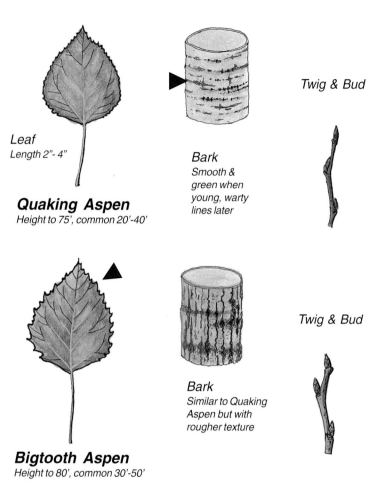

Leaf
Length 2"- 4"

Quaking Aspen
Height to 75', common 20'-40'

Bark
*Smooth &
green when
young, warty
lines later*

Twig & Bud

Bigtooth Aspen
Height to 80', common 30'-50'

Bark
*Similar to Quaking
Aspen but with
rougher texture*

Twig & Bud

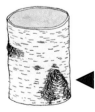

Gray Birch
Height 20'-30'

Bark
*Often with
multiple trunks*

Twig & Bud
*Branches dark to
main trunks*

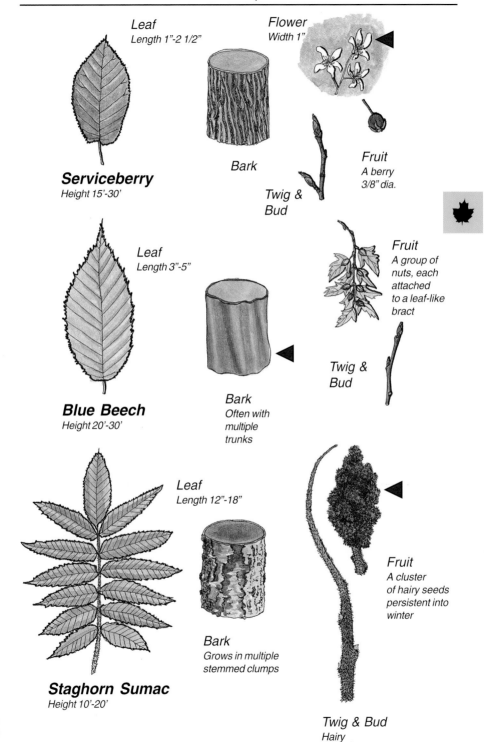

Leaf
Length 1"-2 1/2"

Flower
Width 1"

Bark

Twig &
Bud

Fruit
*A berry
3/8" dia.*

Serviceberry
Height 15'-30'

Leaf
Length 3"-5"

Fruit
*A group of
nuts, each
attached
to a leaf-like
bract*

Twig &
Bud

Blue Beech
Height 20'-30'

Bark
*Often with
multiple
trunks*

Leaf
Length 12"-18"

Fruit
*A cluster
of hairy seeds
persistent into
winter*

Bark
*Grows in multiple
stemmed clumps*

Staghorn Sumac
Height 10'-20'

Twig & Bud
Hairy

Northern Flicker
Length 12 1/2",
Look for white rump
patch when flying

Baltimore Oriole
Length 8 3/4"
Listen for loud melodious
song

Eastern Wood Pewee
Length 6 1/4"
A flycatcher

Ruby-throated Hummingbird
Length 3 3/4"
Listen for buzz of wings

Blackburnian Warbler
Length 5"
Feeds actively through
evergreens

Magnolia Warbler
Length 5 1/2"
Feeds along forest edges

Yellow Warbler
Length 5"
Feeds in shrubs and
small trees

Whip-poor-will
Length 9 3/4" Calls from ground
in forest opening at night

Eastern Towhee
Length 8 1/2"
Scratches through leaves
beneath trees and shrubs

Gray Fox
*Length, body
20"-29", tail 11"-16"*

Striped Skunk
*Length, body 13"-18",
tail 7"-10"*

Track

1 1/2"

1 5/8"

Track

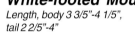

White-footed Mouse
*Length, body 3 3/5"-4 1/5",
tail 2 2/5"-4"*

Track

5/8"

Hairy-tailed Mole
Length, body 4 1/2"-5 1/2", tail 1"-1 1/2"

Snowy Tree Cricket
Length, body 1/2"-5/8"

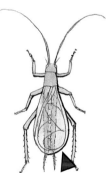

Allegheny Mound Ant
Length, body 1/2"

Ant Mound
Height to 12"

*Adult
Length
1/2"-5/8"*

Six-spotted Green Tiger Beetle

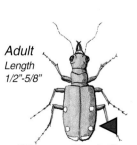

*Empty nymphal
skin*

*Adult
Length
1"-1 1/4"
Wingspan to 3"*

Periodical Cicada

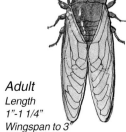

FACTS, TIPS, AND LORE

FACTS, TIPS, AND LORE
SUCCESSIONAL FORESTS

TREES

Quaking Aspen (Trembling Aspen, Popple)

The leaves of a Quaking Aspen tremble in the wind because the *petiole* (the leaf stalk) is flat. This tree is a favorite of the Beaver and also loved by the Porcupine, Ruffed Grouse, and many other birds. In spring look for warblers, goldfinches, and orioles feeding on the *catkins* (caterpillar-shaped clusters of tiny flowers or fruits). The wood is preferred for high-grade *excelsior* (a shredded wood packing material common in the days before styrafoam).

Bigtooth Aspen

Bigtooth Aspen is similar to Quaking Aspen but its leaves are larger, appear later, and have larger teeth along the leaf margin. Unless you look closely at the leaves, you might not realize the two trees are different species.

Gray Birch

Gray Birch grows in a multi-trunk form that is sought after for landscaping, but it is prone to *'browning out'* due to attack by the Birch Leaf Miner, an insect pest. It is one of the first trees to invade open areas, but it is short-lived. Declining trees, covered with fungi, are often outpaced by maples and cherries in a maturing forest.

Serviceberry (Shadbush)

Serviceberry is a showy flowering tree that blooms in spring before any leaves appear. It offers a native landscaping alternative to the Flowering Crabapple, and it blooms earlier. It is a great tree to watch for birds feeding on the ripening berries in June.

American Crabapple (not illustrated)

This apple is one of the few native apples. The fruit is small and tart, and known better as ammunition for apple fights than for eating. Most of the apples found in successional forests are escapees from cultivation by early farmers and settlers.

Staghorn Sumac

Staghorn Sumac grows in masses that are taller in the center and taper down at the edges. These masses can mark the location of an old homestead since they often grow by foundations and barn ruins. Fruit clusters persist into winter and make a good food reserve for wintering birds and they can also be made into a lemonade-like drink.

Blue Beech (Musclewood)

The sinewy bark of this tree looks like highly developed muscles. Although the bark is smooth like beech bark, the tree is more closely related to birches.

HERBACEOUS PLANTS

Blackberry (not illustrated), Raspberries (not illustrated)

Anyone that risks being ravaged by the impressive thorns of the Blackberry to get at the delicious fruit knows how ephemeral these patches are. Blackberries and Raspberries invade disturbed areas but are quickly overshadowed by successional growth. Seeds are spread by birds and mammals after passing through their digestive tracts. Over 150 species of birds and almost all mammals eat the berries.

FERNS

Hay-scented Fern (not illustrated)

This light green fern grows in large colonies in openings in the successional forest. Walk through a colony late in summer to best appreciate the fresh, hay-like scent of this fern. Hay-scented Fern, Sensitive Fern, and Bracken Fern are the only 3 species of ferns that are not protected by New York State law against collecting.

MAMMALS

Gray Fox

The Gray Fox breeds in the spring, and dens in hollow logs or trees, or often in a ground burrow in a dry bank. Young are born in March or April. The most important food for this fox may be the Cottontail Rabbit, but it also eats fruits and nuts of forest trees, small mammals, birds, and insects.

Hairy-tailed Mole

The Hairy-tailed Mole is one of the makers of those underground runways that you find just below the weed mat. Moles paralyze earthworms by biting them and they sometimes store them for later feeding.

Striped Skunk

This well-known member of the weasel family can spray its scent up to 12 feet. If your pet gets too close, try this:

2 pints	Hydrogen Peroxide
¼ cup	Baking Soda
2 Tbsp.	Liquid Dish Detergent

Prepare just before using.
Bathe pet in the mixture, leave on for 15 minutes.
Rinse thoroughly.

The coloration pattern of a Striped Skunk is variable; some are almost all black, others are nearly all white. The skunk dens in burrows and sleeps most of the winter, but it does not hibernate. On warm, late winter days skunk tracks start to appear in the snow as males search out females to breed.

BIRDS

Eastern Towhee

The official common name of the Eastern Towhee was changed recently from its former name, the *Rufous-sided Towhee*. Listen for the male singing a cheerful *'drink your teaee'* from the top of a tree or shrub in spring. The towhee's bulky nest is firmly built of leaves, bark strips, and weed stalks and lined with fine grasses and sometimes hair, on or near the ground under or in a small shrub.

Baltimore Oriole

The Baltimore Oriole was named after Lord Baltimore, whose family colors were black and orange, like the bird's plumage. This neotropical migrant is a bird that adapts well to towns and villages, nesting in the village trees. The female returns about a week or two later than the male. Listen for the male singing from a treetop in the territory he has selected for nesting. The nest is a marvel of construction, a woven pouch slung from a high branch in a tall maple or other street tree. The oriole feeds on insects, flower nectar and sometimes flowers themselves, as well as small seeds. An oriole can be attracted to a feeder with fruit such as orange halves.

Whip-poor-will

The Whip-poor-will has a wide mouth flanked by hairs that is an adaptation for catching insects on the wing.

Ruby-throated Hummingbird

The buzz and squeak of a hummingbird is often heard before the bird is seen. A hummingbird will buzz a colorful shirt or hat, particularly if it is red. Look for the bird hovering near any colorful, tube-shaped flower, but especially red flowers, sipping the flower's nectar. The bird will also eat small gnats, flies, and spiders. A male will engage an intruder in its territory in an animated *'dogfight'*.

Northern Flicker

Watch for this bird feasting on ants at an anthill or a patch of bare ground. The flicker is often heard drumming on a dead branch to attract a mate. A flicker chisels cavities in dead branches for nesting; later these old nest holes are used by many species of birds, mammals, and insects.

Yellow Warbler

Look for a flash of yellow in and around old orchards and cow pastures with thorn apples in bloom for this neotropical migrant. Wet areas and willow swales are other good habitats. The red stripes on the breast of the male are variable and in some birds may be entirely absent. The song of this bird is a clear and rapid, *'sweet sweet sweet i'm so sweet'*.

Magnolia Warbler

This neotropical migrant occupies the late successional forest, especially stands with scattered softwoods. Spring is the best time to see this warbler and other warbler species as they migrate through in large numbers, heading toward nesting sites farther north. Song is a whistled *'weety-weety-weeto'*.

Blackburnian Warbler

The Blackburnian Warbler is one of the most colorful members of the warbler family. A neotropical migrant, it can be seen during spring migration, high in the treetops of the late successional forest habitat, working the leaves and branch tips for insects.

INSECTS

Periodical Cicada

Listen for the buzz of the cicada from the treetops in summer. The cicada nymph develops in the ground, feeding on tree sap for 13-17 years before emerging. The nymph finally matures and crawls up a tree trunk where it splits its skin and emerges as an adult. The adult lives only long enough to breed and deposit eggs in a slit in tree bark. When the young hatch they burrow into the soil to complete the cycle.

Allegheny Mound Ant (Red Ant)

This is the ant that is responsible for the mounds found in openings in the forest. This ant will also take over a stack of lumber or pile of debris, transport millions of pieces of leaves, twigs, and wood and pack it into all the spaces. When disturbed, the colony emits an offensive odor. The audacious soldiers rear on their hind legs and confront any attacker, even a person.

SHRUBLANDS

VERIFYING CHARACTERISTICS

- Clumps of Shrubs of the Same Species
- Bands of Shrubs Along edges of Fields, Rivers, and Wet Areas
- Few Trees of any Size

Nature

The sun's rays diffuse light above the
eastern hill.
Cues nature's awakening through the
warbler's trill.

The misty fog hovers, concealing all in a
nebulous veil.
Gradually dissipating, dissolving and
leaving no trail.

Drops of dew sparkle like diamonds
clinging to a frond.
Morning breezes stir the mirrored
surface of a pond.

Vivid impressions of solitude I treasure
so much.
I long that they will be there for all
hearts to touch.

John R. Cecil

Shrublands present a barrier to the movement of people that can be as effective as a solid wall. This *brush*, as it is called without affection, is usually targeted for removal by people, but it is valued by many species. When the forest cover is removed from an area by a natural force or people, it will be invaded by herbaceous plants, vines, and shrubs competing vigorously for every square inch of soil. Shrub habitats that grow after a disturbance are temporary stages in succession from field to forest. Once the pioneer tree species close the canopy over an area, the sun-loving plants die out and you can once again walk through the woods. Just try forcing your way through a shrub thicket in late summer when the underbrush is at its most vigorous stage, and you will realize why this habitat is so important for many species of birds and mammals. It offers protection and cover for nesting, as well as a steady source of seeds, berries, and insects for food.

Spring

Shrublands are a great place to see migrating warblers. Look for them early in the season, before the leaves break out of bud, to see those that are just passing through. Watch for mating activity at the same time by the birds that will nest in the shrubs. Once the leaves come out and the birds are nesting, seeing more than a colorful flash will be a challenge. Listen for the **Chestnut-sided Warbler** singing; *'please, please, please to meetcha'* from the top of a branch.

There is a spectacle in the spring hayfields that is a treat to hear and watch if you have good eyesight at dusk. After the ground has thawed, but before the grasses are growing, listen for a *'pneent'* sound repeated at short intervals. After a short time the sound will change to a rapid, high-pitched *'chirp'* fading into the sky. As the *'chirp'* fades from hearing, it is replaced by a sweeping *'wheeep-weep-weep-weep'* that grows louder until it suddenly stops, and the *'pneent'* is heard again. The **American Woodcock**, also called the *Timber Doodle*, a shorebird that has forsaken its ancestral haunt of marsh and shore for the upland habitat, performs these audio antics. The performance is a mating ritual, and experiencing it is a rite of spring for people who know where and when to look.

Summer

Summer is the time when shrublands display their glory in the form of flowers. Watch the progression of blooms from the creamy whites of the **Viburnums** to the blues, pinks, yellows, and almost every other color of the herbaceous plants that create a giant bouquet by late summer. The herbaceous plants are most easily identified when they are flowering.

Find a group of milkweeds, plants with circular holes in the leaves are the best bet, and search the undersides of the leaves for the gem-like *chrysalis* (cocoon-like structure) of the **Monarch Butterfly**. The large, bright yellow, white, and black striped Monarch caterpillar makes the structure. The Monarch caterpillar feeds only on milkweed and when it is ready to pupate, it attaches itself to the leaf and wraps itself in a hard, green sheath with a gold-tipped crown. The adult Monarch emerges from the chrysalis after a period of metamorphosis. You can find a milkweed leaf with a chrysalis attached, put it into a shoe box with one side screened and watch the process. There is a tale that the caterpillar can sting and is poisonous to touch. Not so for humans, but to birds it is a different story. The caterpillar, while feeding on milkweed, picks up the poison (all milky sap plants contain plant poisons) from the plant and retains it even as a butterfly. Both the caterpillars and butterflies are distasteful to birds and make them sick.

Look out at a field of **Goldenrod** in late summer, and you will notice that many individuals have a round protuberance part way up the stem. This bump is called a *gall,* and it is the result of an interaction between the Goldenrod and a small fly called the **Goldenrod Gall Fly.** The fly lays its eggs on the young stem and when the larvae hatches, it burrows into the living plant tissue. The plant responds by depositing layers of tissue around the fly's chamber, creating the round gall. The plant easily survives and provides a winter retreat for the developing fly. If you examine these galls on the dead winter stems of the Goldenrod, you will notice that many show the tiny round emergence hole of the fly. Others are broken apart by winter birds that feed on the larvae, such as chickadees and woodpeckers. Galls are a common expression of the numerous interactions between insects and plants. Goldenrod is particularly prone to gall making insects; besides the Gall Fly, a moth produces an elliptical gall on the stem and a midge produces a bunch gall in the leaf buds.

Go out into the field on a warm summer evening and you will see it decorated with sparkling flashes of light from the **Lightning Bug,** or *Firefly.* This soft-bodied beetle produces a chemical light with a substance called *luciferin.* The substance is stored in the beetle's belly in special cells surrounded by other cells that serve to reflect and intensify the light, allowing it to control the pattern of the light flashes. The male uses the light as it flies about as a signal to the female. The female responds with a flash of its own, usually from a perch, drawing the male to it. There are several species of fireflies on Tug Hill, each with its own specific sequence, intensity, and duration of light flashes. Fireflies eat other insects and sometimes will even eat each other. The female of one species of firefly uses her light-making ability to attract the males of other species. When they arrive she promptly devours them.

Fall

Shrublands are among the first habitats to show signs of fall. In late August the **Dogwoods** already begin to change color. After the first frost many of the herbaceous plants turn black and wither. Still, between the brilliant flower heads of the herbaceous plants and the brilliant fall leaves of the woody shrubs, the beautiful display retains its glory.

Winter

When the first heavy snows come you can finally venture into the shrublands, but only with snowshoes. Many mammals find cover and tender bark beneath the snow-arched caverns. Many species of birds also use shrublands for nesting cover. Look for nests among the shrub masses early in winter. Each species of bird uses different materials and techniques to build a nest, making it possible, with a little study, to identify the nester.

ILLUSTRATIONS

Leaf
Length 2"-9"
Shape variable

**Twig &
Bud**
Twigs spicy
aromatic when
broken

Sassafras

Height varies from a thicket of low shrubs to a
medium size tree

Leaf
Length 1"-3"

**Twig &
Bud**

Fruit 1/8"
Persistent
into winter

Steeplebush

Height 2'-4'

Flower
July-August
Clusters 4"-6" tall

Fruit 1/3"
Persistent
into winter

Leaf
Length 2"-3 1/2"
Shiny

**Twig &
Bud**

Red Chokeberry

Height 3'-8'

Flower
April-May
Width 1/2"

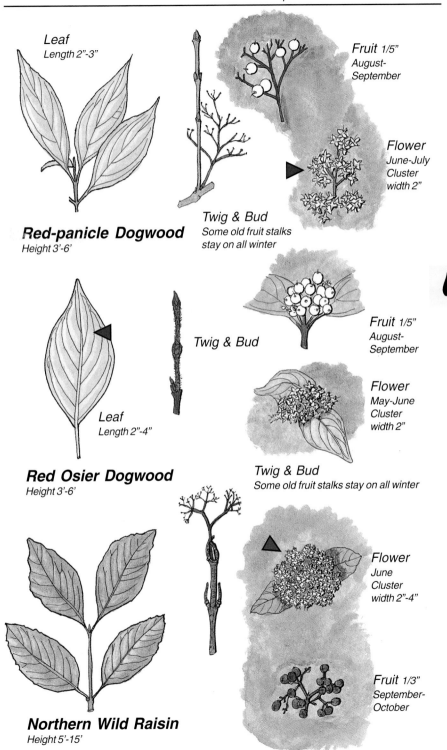

Leaf
Length 2"-3"

Fruit *1/5"*
*August-
September*

Flower
*June-July
Cluster
width 2"*

Red-panicle Dogwood
Height 3'-6'

Twig & Bud
*Some old fruit stalks
stay on all winter*

Twig & Bud

Fruit *1/5"*
*August-
September*

Flower
*May-June
Cluster
width 2"*

Leaf
Length 2"-4"

Red Osier Dogwood
Height 3'-6'

Twig & Bud
Some old fruit stalks stay on all winter

Flower
*June
Cluster
width 2"-4"*

Fruit *1/3"*
*September-
October*

Northern Wild Raisin
Height 5'-15'

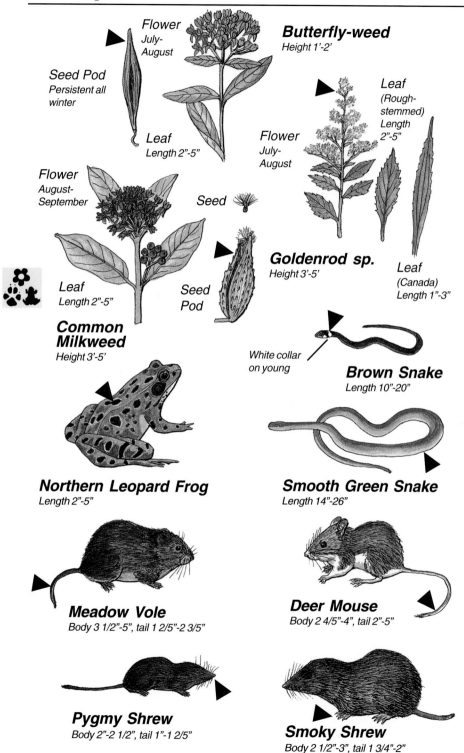

Flower
July-August

Butterfly-weed
Height 1'-2'

Seed Pod
Persistent all winter

Leaf
Length 2"-5"

Leaf
(Rough-stemmed)
Length 2"-5"

Flower
July-August

Flower
August-September

Seed

Goldenrod sp.
Height 3'-5'

Leaf
Length 2"-5"

Seed
Pod

Leaf
(Canada)
Length 1"-3"

Common Milkweed
Height 3'-5'

White collar
on young

Brown Snake
Length 10"-20"

Northern Leopard Frog
Length 2"-5"

Smooth Green Snake
Length 14"-26"

Meadow Vole
Body 3 1/2"-5", tail 1 2/5"-2 3/5"

Deer Mouse
Body 2 4/5"-4", tail 2"-5"

Pygmy Shrew
Body 2"-2 1/2", tail 1"-1 2/5"

Smoky Shrew
Body 2 1/2"-3", tail 1 3/4"-2"

Chestnut-sided Warbler
Length 5"
Commonly seen in
shrubby areas
before leaves emerge

Rusty-colored
sides

Indigo Bunting
Length 5 1/2"
Male sings late into the
summer

Purple Finch
Length 6"

Heavy bill

Black wings

American Goldfinch
Length 5"
Often seen feeding on thistle

Brown Thrasher
Length 11 1/2"
Song is long and varied, each phrase
repeated three times

Gray Catbird
Length 8 1/2"
Listen for 'meow' from dense brush

White tail
stripes

Long bill

Dark-eyed Junco
Length 6 1/4"
White tail stripes flash when flying

American Woodcock Length 11"
Watch for aerial display at dusk in early spring

Moth (Isabella Tiger Moth) Wingspan 1 5/8"- 2"

Buckeye Wingspan 1 5/8"-2 3/4"

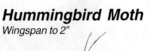

Caterpillar Length to 2 1/4"

Hummingbird Moth Wingspan to 2"

Woolly Bear

Larva in opened gall

Praying Mantis Length 2"-2 1/2"

Spring Azure Wingspan 1 1/8"-1 1/4"

Goldenrod Gall Fly Length 1/4"

Robber Fly Length to 1"

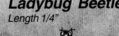

Ladybug Beetle Length 1/4"

Leaf Beetle Length 3/8"

Red Milkweed Beetle Length 1/2"

Ground Beetle Length to 5/8"

Field Cricket Length to 1 1/8"

Larva 'Glowworm'

Lightning Bug Length 1/4"

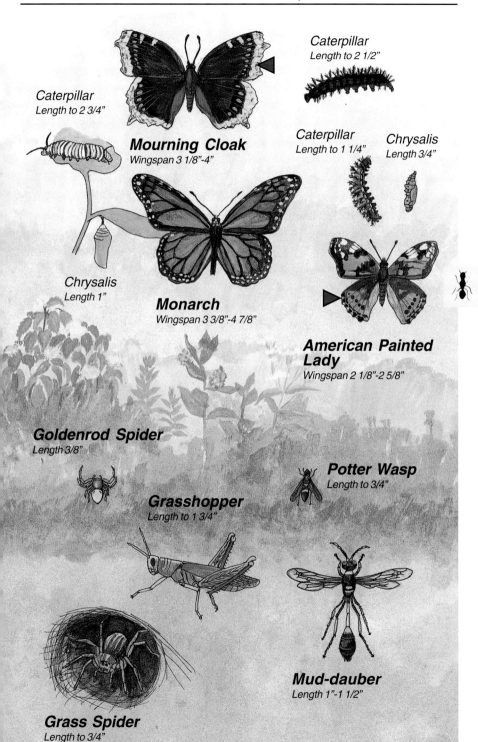

Caterpillar
Length to 2 3/4"

Caterpillar
Length to 2 1/2"

Mourning Cloak
Wingspan 3 1/8"-4"

Caterpillar
Length to 1 1/4"

Chrysalis
Length 3/4"

Chrysalis
Length 1"

Monarch
Wingspan 3 3/8"-4 7/8"

**American Painted
Lady**
Wingspan 2 1/8"-2 5/8"

Goldenrod Spider
Length 3/8"

Potter Wasp
Length to 3/4"

Grasshopper
Length to 1 3/4"

Mud-dauber
Length 1"-1 1/2"

Grass Spider
Length to 3/4"

FACTS, TIPS, AND LORE

FACTS, TIPS, *AND* LORE
SHRUBLANDS

SHRUBS

Highbush Blueberry   (not illustrated)

This blueberry is one of the most widely recognized shrubs on the Hill. There are several different species of blueberries, but Highbush is the tallest, and it has the largest, sweetest fruits. The blueberry is a favorite of wildlife as well as people.

Northern Wild Raisin

The persistent fruits of the wild raisin are an important winter food source for birds. This shrub, with its showy flower cluster and deep red fall color, makes an attractive native ornamental. The fruit clusters are also showy, and they attract birds to the yard.

Red-panicle Dogwood

This shrub of abandoned moist pastures spreads by suckering and forms round clumps that are higher in the middle and taper down on all sides. This dogwood provides food and shelter for deer and many birds, and it is a good native ornamental species for mass plantings.

Steeplebush

This shrubby herbaceous plant forms thickets and tangles and spreads by suckering and adventitious rooting. Steeplebush usually retains some dead flower stalks into the next growing season, giving it a ragged appearance.

HERBACEOUS PLANTS

Common Milkweed, Butterfly-weed

Search the pink flower clusters of the Common Milkweed for a variety of insects, including flies, wasps, beetles, and butterflies. Butterfly-weed also attracts a menagerie of insects, but prefers wetter sites than the Common Milkweed. The milky extract of both plants is poisonous, and Monarchs and other caterpillars that consume it also become poisonous to birds that might eat them.

MAMMALS

Masked Shrew   (not illustrated)

The population of the Masked Shrew is cyclical; some years this shrew is abundant, other years it is scarce. It is active all year. The shrew's high metabolic rate allows it to produce three litters per year, but its life span is short. The Masked Shrew feeds on insect larvae, worms, and tiny mollusks.

Pygmy Shrew

This shrew is so small that its burrow resembles that of a large earthworm. The Pygmy Shrew feeds on small grubs, worms, beetle larvae, and adult flies.

Short-tailed Shrew   (not illustrated)

Like all shrews, the Short-tailed Shrew has small eyes and concealed ears, but this shrew is stocky, with a blunt muzzle and a short tail. This shrew constructs a nest of clumps of leaves beneath stumps or logs. A young shrew grows quickly and matures in its first year. The Short-tailed Shrew feeds on invertebrates, small salamanders, small mammals, and even small birds, but worms and snails are its most important prey. A shrew has a strong scent that causes predators to avoid it; this scent is often the first clue that a shrew has been caught in a mousetrap. A shrew also makes a variety of vocalizations, from ultrasonic sounds to squeaks and clicks. A shrew may be heard signaling to a companion in the ground litter by people with keen hearing.

Meadow Vole (Meadow Mouse)

The Meadow Voles is more closely related to the muskrat and lemming than it is to any of our other native rodents. Voles are an important food source for kestrels, owls, and hawks.

BIRDS

Brown Thrasher

The Brown Thrasher is a large and conspicuous bird. Though the bird's color is not distinct, its song is robust and dominating.

INSECTS AND OTHER INVERTEBRATES

Mourning Cloak

The Mourning Cloak is named for the somber color of the black funeral shawl worn by widows. This butterfly can be seen in mid-winter, during thaws, as the adult moves to another wintering location. The Mourning Cloak lives about 10-11 months, longer than any other butterfly on the Hill. The larvae of this butterfly feed together in a silk web at first, but later feed alone or in small groups. Mourning Cloak caterpillars feed on birch, elm, poplar, aspen, and willow.

Monarch

Monarchs migrate south to Mexico in the fall, and after wintering in masses of thousands of butterflies, they begin the move north. During the trip, the butterflies mate, lay eggs on Common Milkweed, and die. The eggs hatch, the caterpillar eats the Milkweed leaves and forms a chrysalis. A new adult emerges from the chrysalis and continues the migration north to repeat the cycle. Several generations may pass before the Monarch appears on the Hill each year.

Viceroy (not illustrated)

The Viceroy mimics the Monarch but is usually smaller in size. Like the Monarch, it is also distasteful and emetic to birds. If a bird eats either butterfly, it will not only avoid the one it ate, but also the look-alike. The caterpillar also uses mimicry for defense, but it has chosen a less colorful object to copy; it looks like a bird dropping.

Spring Azure (Common Blue)

The Spring Azure is a small but bright butterfly appearing early in spring. This butterfly feeds on the early cherry blossoms and later on viburnum blossoms.

Question Mark (not illustrated)

A silver comma and dot forming a *'question mark'* on the underside of the hind wing gives this species its name. The Question Mark has two forms, a summer and a winter form. In winter, the adult has blue bordered wings with black and brown undersides. In summer, the adult's hind wings are dark with violet undersides. Young larvae feed in a group, then become loners as they grow older. The caterpillar feeds on False Nettle and elm. The butterfly feeds on rotting fruit and sap. The male perches on a tree branch and chases other males and larger insects away.

American Painted Lady

Try to see the undersides of the wings of this butterfly as it feeds. The intricate pattern of lines and circles looks like a work of abstract art.

Isabella Tiger Moth

This moth is known best to us in its larval stage as the Woolly Bear Caterpillar. The larvae eat many plants, including asters, birches, clover, corn, elms, maples, and sunflowers. The colors of the caterpillar change as it molts, becoming less black and more reddish with age. Using the color patterns as an indication of the severity of the upcoming winter is not supported by science but may be just as accurate as any other method.

Hummingbird Moth

Look for this bee-sized, daytime moth hovering by flowers, sipping nectar like a hummingbird. The White-lined Sphinx, the larger of the two common species, has a wingspan of up to 3 ½ inches.

Ladybug Beetle

The Ladybug Beetle (*Ladybug*) is a favorite insect of many people. It is attractive to the eye with its spotted red back, and it is among the most beneficial of insects. Both the adults and larvae are predators of scale insects, aphids, mites, weevils, and the larvae of other beetles that are injurious to crops.

Praying Mantis

The familiar Praying Mantis is included in the group of insects known as mantids, but this large mantid is an alien. The Praying Mantis is a major carnivore that grabs its prey with powerful foreclaws. Not even her mate escapes her clutch, since she concludes the mating act when she consumes him.

Crickets and Grasshoppers

These insects are very common and well known for their jumping ability. Grasshoppers and locusts eat plants while crickets have wider diets and are not above scavenging other insects. Both creatures sing by rubbing their wings or legs together.

Spiders

Although all spiders do not spin webs, they all make silk, and web spinning is the hallmark of this group. All spiders are predatory and feed on prey they overpower by injecting a powerful poison that paralyzes the victim and liquefies its insides at the same time. There are no spiders native to the Tug Hill that possess toxins capable of killing the average person, but a few may bite and produce necrotic tissue damage.

Wolf and Nursery-web Spiders vigorously seek out prey animals. Both of these large spiders have very hairy bodies and the females carry their egg sac around under their bodies. They are passive hunters that wait in hiding for their prey to pass by and then pounce. Some, such as the Funnel Web Spiders, use silk to create a hiding place, while others wait in places that match their body color. The yellow Goldenrod Spider sits in yellow flowers and captures pollinating insects. Look for it on Goldenrod flowers. Other spiders build a web of sticky silk that acts as a trap for flying insects.

Spider silk is extremely strong and has the ability to stretch without breaking. There are many variations in spider webs, but most are either orb webs like those used by the large Black-and-yellow Garden Spider, two-dimensional sheet webs, or the more irregular, three dimensional scaffold-type web made by the common cellar spider and house spider so often found in our homes.

Dry Run - Coyote

Painting by Robert McNamara

FARMLANDS

VERIFYING CHARACTERISTICS

- Open Land in Active Agriculture
- Field Crops, Active Pasture, or Fallow Fields
- Absence of Woody Plant Growth in Open Areas

"Dairy farming on the Hill is a never ending challenge,
with its harsh winters and thin soils, yet its stark, unique
beauty, abundance of wild life and fisheries, combined
with Tug Hill's vast forests has always made it the place
I want to raise my family"

Tim LeVan

There is more to see in fields and pastures than cows. Any farmer will tell you about the fascinating things that can be seen from the seat of a tractor. The energy expended by settlers in clearing the forest for agriculture can be appreciated by anyone who has dug out a stump by hand or cleared a field of the spring crop of stones. Open landscapes were a minor part of the original cover on the Hill, yet the pastoral scenery common to many locations has become the desired vision of many residents and visitors. At one time much of the Hill was cleared, but today the forest is regenerating as farms are abandoned. Take advantage of the scarce areas that are still open and scan the fields with binoculars or a scope. Open areas offer many opportunities for watching wildlife and for seeing many plants, insects, reptiles, and other creatures not found elsewhere on the Hill.

Many plants found in fallow fields, along roadsides, and in unplanted spaces are *aliens* or *exotics* (plants that are not native to the area, or perhaps the continent) such as Common Burdock and Queen- Anne's-Lace. Immigrants brought many plants to this continent for medicinal or cooking uses, and they brought many others unintentionally. Some exotics have become nuisances because there are no natural controls on their growth. In some cases, exotics can crowd out native species and cover large areas while offering little value for wildlife or people.

117

Hedgerows usually divide the wide-open spaces of croplands. In addition to their value in controlling soil erosion and buffering winds, hedgerows are great places to look for wildlife on farms. The stone walls that are a common component of hedgerows hide chipmunks and other rodents, and make a good hunting place for predators. Migrating songbirds use the shelter of hedgerows to safely cross open fields and find food along the way. Deer and other large mammals use hedgerows as corridors to move stealthily from field to woods and back.

Spring

A favorite early spring leisure time activity for Hill residents is watching **White-tailed Deer**. When the spring sunshine finally starts burning holes in the snow pack on the fields, deer come out of their wintering *yards* (specific places where deer find shelter during the depths of winter) and seek out the grasses and herbaceous plants that were hidden under the snow. Herds of 50 deer are not uncommon. Deer are most often seen around sunrise and sunset, but they can be seen at almost any time of the day when the conditions are right for foraging.

The welcome return of the **Eastern Bluebird**, the state bird of New York, is most evident when a pair has nested, early in spring, and the birds are busy rearing young. After years of decline, the unmistakable flash of striking blue is once again a common sight near farmlands. The Eastern Bluebird population can be enhanced with a little help from people by providing properly designed and maintained bluebird boxes to protect the birds from competition from introduced species like Starlings and House Sparrows. The song of the Eastern Bluebird is a simple musical '*chur-wi*' of three or four gurgling notes, often sung while flying overhead during migration.

Migrating hawks, especially the **Red-tailed Hawk**, begin to arrive from their southern winter areas in March and April. Despite its nickname, the *Chicken Hawk*, this hawk eats far more rodents like woodchucks and rabbits than chickens, making it a farmer's ally instead of an enemy. Look for this large hawk perched in hedgerows or soaring over fields searching for rodents. Its large nest of sticks can often be found in the crotch of a tall tree in a small wood lot surrounded by fields, or in a hedgerow. The nests are easy to spot before the leaves come out. In April check the nest for a bump in the middle, the back and head of the hen can usually be seen when the bird is sitting on eggs. By the first of June the young birds, now almost as large as the adults, sit tall on the edge of the nest. Watch from a distance with binoculars or a spotting scope so the nest will not be disturbed.

Summer

What causes that frothy white spit on the stems of many meadow plants? This perpetual bubble-bath is the unusual home of the nymph of the Spittlebug or *Froghopper*; a tiny insect common in all cleared areas of Tug Hill. The adult lays eggs on the stems of plants in summer or fall, where the eggs remain over winter. In spring, the eggs hatch and the tiny nymph immediately begins to create the spittle. It does so first by positioning itself upside down, piercing the stem, and sucking up plant juices. Excess juice is excreted out its anus and whipped into a sticky froth as it pours over its body. It is not known for sure, but it is believed the froth is distasteful to would-be predators. At least one species of fly lays its eggs in the froth so that its larvae will also get this measure of protection. Several common species of spittlebugs are found on Tug Hill; one uses grasses, a second is found on clover and alfalfa, while a third prefers pine, fir, and hemlock.

Open fields are the only places where you can see two colorful and musical birds, the **Eastern Meadowlark** and the **Bobolink**. These birds are dependent upon a grassland habitat for feeding and nesting. The male Bobolink has a conspicuous black and white plumage pattern, and patrols its territory with a fluttering flight. The Eastern Meadowlark displays a white tail patch when it flies in a *'wingbeat and glide'* pattern. Listen for the meadowlark singing its melodious song from a fence post or hay bale at midday.

It is doubtful that there is a creature on the entire Hill that has more myths, tall tales, and misguided notions about it than the **Eastern Milk Snake**. The tallest tale is the one that gave the snake its common name; that it sneaks into a barn and sucks the milk from the teats of a cow. The snake can be seen in a barn, but it is looking for rodents or insects, not milk. This snake is often called the *Spotted Adder* after the venomous serpent of Europe and Asia, probably due to its slightly unnerving habit of vibrating its tail like a rattlesnake when annoyed, and because many assume any boldly-patterned snake is poisonous. The Eastern Milk Snake is harmless; in fact, it performs a valuable service to farmers by consuming small mammals that might otherwise damage crops.

Winter

On a clear, still winter night it is now common to hear the howl of the **Eastern Coyote**. Some may find the call eerie, but it reminds others of the wilderness. Contrary to some suspicions, the coyote does not typically kill livestock or game animals. The coyote usually preys on rodents, rabbit, and winter-killed deer. While the coyote was formerly considered a loner, on the Hill it seems to be adapting to life in a pack. A pack of coyotes rests more, travels less, and has a smaller home range in winter than would the same number of animals living alone or in pairs, thus conserving energy.

Coyotes are able to kill larger prey, like winter-weakened deer, by hunting cooperatively. The general health of the deer population may be strengthened by having the weak animals culled from the herd. Look for a coyote at dusk and dawn patrolling the fields for rodents. It stalks a foraging mouse, carefully cocks its ears forward, and listens for the exact location of its prey. When it pinpoints the victim, the coyote leaps almost straight up and pounces down to pin the mouse with its front paws. When a coyote catches a mouse, it often tosses it in the air a time or two before it swallows it whole.

Reports of occasional visits to the hen house have given the **Short-tailed Weasel**, or *Ermine*, a bad reputation. However, most farmers recognize the benefits of having this small predator around the farm to control the population of rodent pests. Some farmers have found chickens or other animals killed, with much of the blood drained out of them, and this has created a myth that the weasel sucks the blood of its victim. Sometimes the weasel kills by a bite to the back of the neck, and when it does so, perhaps the jugular is severed; this would cause rapid and enormous loss of blood from the victim, which the weasel could then lick up for a relatively filling meal. However, meat and bone are the most important components of the weasel's diet. Studies of weasel stomachs have shown that mice account for over 95 percent of their diet. Watch for the hyperactive weasel along a hedgerow, stone wall, or a thicket where it can catch field mice, voles, chipmunks, and even Snowshoe Hares.

The open country typical of farmlands is a good place to see a **Snowy Owl**. Sighting a snowy is a treat enjoyed only in certain winters when severe weather and a low lemming population forces owls further south in search of food than they would normally venture. Look for this large white owl on a fence post, telephone pole, or in a wide open field, *mantling* (covering a catch with hunched wings) its rodent prey.

Winter Light - Short-tailed Weasel (Ermine)

ILLUSTRATIONS

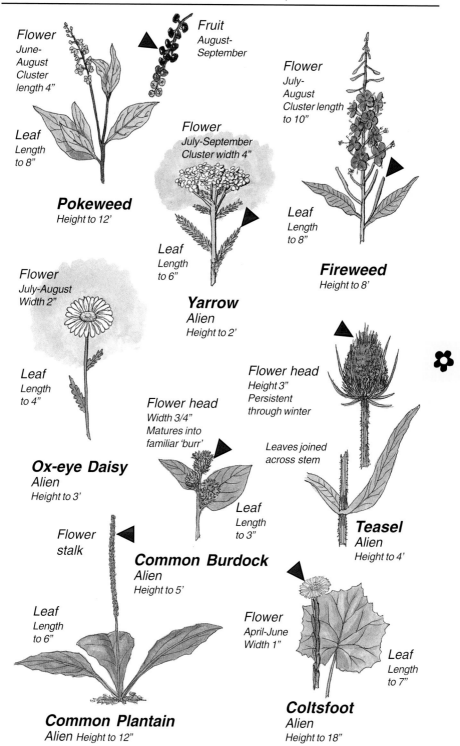

Flower
June-
August
Cluster
length 4"

Fruit
August-
September

Leaf
Length
to 8"

Pokeweed
Height to 12'

Flower
July-September
Cluster width 4"

Leaf
Length
to 6"

Yarrow
Alien
Height to 2'

Flower
July-
August
Cluster length
to 10"

Leaf
Length
to 8"

Fireweed
Height to 8'

Flower
July-August
Width 2"

Leaf
Length
to 4"

Ox-eye Daisy
Alien
Height to 3'

Flower head
Width 3/4"
Matures into
familiar 'burr'

Leaf
Length
to 3"

Common Burdock
Alien
Height to 5'

Flower head
Height 3"
Persistent
through winter

*Leaves joined
across stem*

Teasel
Alien
Height to 4'

**Flower
stalk**

Leaf
Length
to 6"

Common Plantain
Alien Height to 12"

Flower
April-June
Width 1"

Leaf
Length
to 7"

Coltsfoot
Alien
Height to 18"

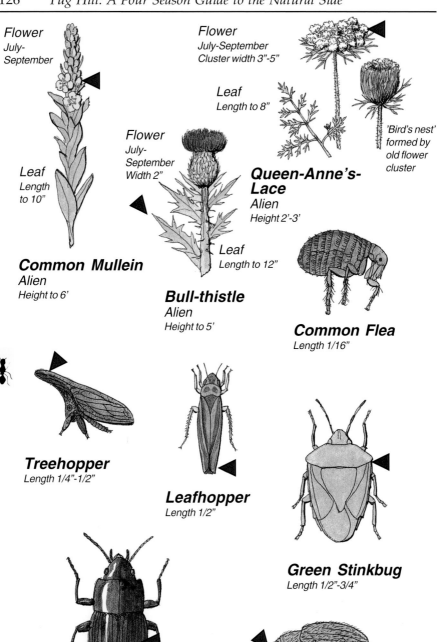

Flower
July-September

Leaf
Length to 10"

Common Mullein
Alien
Height to 6'

Flower
July-September
Width 2"

Leaf
Length to 12"

Bull-thistle
Alien
Height to 5'

Flower
July-September
Cluster width 3"-5"

Leaf
Length to 8"

Queen-Anne's-Lace
Alien
Height 2'-3'

'Bird's nest' formed by old flower cluster

Common Flea
Length 1/16"

Treehopper
Length 1/4"-1/2"

Leafhopper
Length 1/2"

Green Stinkbug
Length 1/2"-3/4"

Ground Beetle
Length 1/2"-5/8"

Weevil
Height 1/8"-1/4"

Eastern Milk Snake
Length to 26"-52"

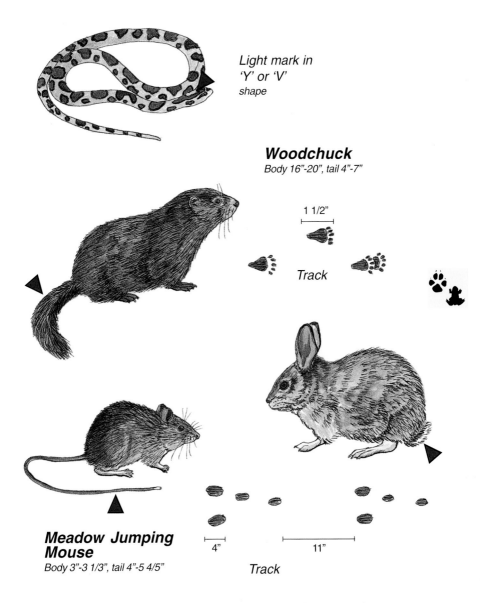

Light mark in
'Y' or 'V'
shape

Woodchuck
Body 16"-20", tail 4"-7"

1 1/2"

Track

Meadow Jumping
Mouse
Body 3"-3 1/3", tail 4"-5 4/5"

4"

11"

Track

Eastern Cottontail
Body 14"-17", tail 2 1/2"-3"

Ring-billed Gull
Length 18"-20",
Wingspan 48"-49"

Black ring around bill

Scissor tail

Barn Swallow
Length 6 3/4"
Perches in groups on wires

Eastern Phoebe
Length 7"
Nests on ledges
on buildings
Call a raspy
'fee-bee'

Snowy Owl
Length 23"
Most often seen
in the coldest
part of winter

Double band on neck

Killdeer
Length 10 1/2"
Pretends to be injured to
decoy intruders from nest

Canada Goose
Length 25"-45"
Grazes in cornfields
in spring and fall

American Kestrel
*Length 10 1/2",
Wingspan 24"
Hovers over
potential
prey*

Red-tailed Hawk
*Length 20"-24",
Wingspan 46"-54"
Perches in
hedgerows*

Eastern Bluebird
*Length 7" Most easily seen
near nest boxes*

Bobolink
*Length 7"
Bubbling song often
given in flight*

Black throat
patch

Mourning Dove
*Length 12"
Feeds on the ground,
call is owl-like*

Eastern Meadowlark
*Length 9 1/2"
Sings from a fence post or hay bale*

FACTS, TIPS, AND LORE

FACTS, TIPS, AND LORE
FARMLANDS

HERBACEOUS PLANTS

Yarrow (Milfoil)

Crush a fresh Yarrow leaf and you will notice a strong medicinal smell. The plant is used for bruises, wounds, burns, and can be chewed to relieve toothache.

Common Burdock

This familiar plant of roadsides and fields was the inspiration for Velcro. The clinging of the hooked *burs* is a method used by the plant to disperse its seeds. The young leaves and roots are edible, and the plant has many medicinal applications including use as an external antiseptic.

Ox-Eye Daisy

Take a close look at the head of this familiar plant of fields and roadsides; it is actually composed of many flowers. There are sterile white ray flowers, the *'petals'* we pluck to decide if he or she loves us or not, and hundreds of fertile yellow disk flowers. The young leaves of this plant are good in a salad, though they have a strong taste.

Bull-thistle

Farmers curse this well-armed plant. Bull-thistle's rose-purple flowers produce sweet nectar that the sharp spines protect from nectar thieves. Butterflies are primary pollinators and the goldfinch enjoys the thistle seed and uses the thistle down to line its nests. It is the national flower of Scotland. Legend has it that during the Danish invasion a Dane stepped on a thistle and cried out, alerting the sleeping Scots.

Queen-Anne's-Lace

The familiar flat flower clusters of this wild member of the cultivated carrot family are composed of up to 500 individual flowers. The central purple petals symbolize a drop of Queen Anne's blood from the finger she pricked while making lace. After flowering, the flower cluster takes on a hollow nest shape, giving it another of its names, *Bird's Nest*.

Teasel

Study the prickly cone-shaped flowerheads of this roadside plant. Early textile processors found that the stiff bracts were great for raising the nap of wool, or teasing cloth. Cultivation of Teasel was an important industry in New York, and it was only fairly recently that the function of the heads was replaced by machinery. It is said that the finish of the machined cloth is not as luxurious as when it was teased with Teasel.

Fireweed

Any site with a dense stand of this plant with its brilliant magenta flowers has probably been burned recently, hence the name Fireweed. Young Fireweed shoots and leaves are edible, similar to asparagus and spinach, respectively, and the older leaves can be used as tea. Fireweed has also been used medicinally for respiratory problems.

Pokeweed

You can identify this plant with your nose. Pokeweed is a foul-smelling weed common in fields, yards, and roadsides. It becomes more conspicuous in late summer because of its large size and showy purple fruit. It is the ingredient of poke salad, but certain parts of the plant become poisonous when older, so it is best to only enjoy it visually.

Common Plantain

This common weed of lawn and roadside is an alien to our continent. Common Plantain came here with the colonists and went everywhere they did, earning it the name *White-man's Footprint* from native people. Common Plantain was used to help stop bleeding, and as a remedy for burns, cuts, insect bites, and inflammations.

Common Mullein

This curious field plant is a *biennial* plant (it matures over two seasons). Common Mullein draws attention to itself in the second year of growth when it sends up a tall flowering stalk that bears bright sulfur-yellow flowers. The whole plant, except the flowers, is covered with whitish-gray fuzz. The fuzz repels grazing animals by irritating their mucous membranes, and it protects the plant from moisture loss and extremes of sunlight and cold. *Candlewick Plant* and *Torches* are two other common names that come from use of the felt for lamp wicks, and use of the entire flowering stalk as a torch after dipping it in suet. Mullein leaves have been used to rub ladies' cheeks as a sort of country rouge, and to line shoes to keep the wearer's feet warm.

Coltsfoot

This alien plant is often seen in ditches in early spring when its dandelion-like flowers appear before the leaves. The leaves are shaped like a horse's footprint, hence its name. The tuft of silky hairs on the seeds is often used by the goldfinch to line its nest.

MOSSES AND FERNS

Twisted Cord Moss   (not illustrated)

Look for this moss in highly disturbed areas. It invades burned areas due to the increased availability of certain nutrients. The plant is small and bright green, but the spore-bearing stalk (the twisted cord) is a reddish color.

MAMMALS

White-tailed Deer

White-tailed Deer migrate from their summer range to winter yards. In the yards the deer find shelter and less snow beneath evergreen trees. They pack herd paths between nearby water holes and browse to make moving easier. When the snow is deep and deer are *'yarded up'*, it is critical to keep your dog on a leash to keep it from chasing the deer out of their yards and jeopardizing their winter survival. Fawns are born in May and June; their camouflaged bodies disappear in brushy cover. The female deer often leaves the fawn alone while she feeds, depending upon the cover for protection. An *'abandoned'* fawn is not usually far from its mother and should be left alone.

Woodchuck

Legend says that if the Woodchuck (*Groundhog*) sees its shadow on February 2nd when it emerges from its burrow, it will go back into hibernation for 6 more weeks of winter. The Woodchuck is a true hibernator. It does not store food for winter use. It sleeps through winter, lowering its body temperature and metabolic rate, and depends entirely on its fat reserves. Succeeding generations of Woodchucks may use and enlarge their ancestral den. Other animals will also share the same den, including the Opossum, Raccoon, and Cottontail Rabbit, as well as various shrews, mice, and voles. Foxes have also been found in Woodchuck dens. The Woodchuck has many predators, not the least of which are people.

Eastern Cottontail

The female cottontail digs a nest hole and lines it with grass or other soft vegetation and a heavy layer of fur plucked from her belly or side. Cottontails are one of the premier game animals in the United States. The pelt is used for clothing and the meat is considered by many to be a delicacy. Tug Hill is at the northern extent of the cottontail range.

Long-tailed Weasel , Short-tailed Weasel (Ermine)

Two species of weasels, the Long-tailed Weasel and the Ermine, or Short-tailed Weasel, are found on the Hill. Both are brown in summer (Apr-Oct), and turn white in winter (beginning Nov-Dec). Weasels are very active animals, and can be seen at any time of the day or night, but are most often observed in the late afternoon, evening, and early morning.

Meadow Jumping Mouse

This mouse lives in dense, tall grasses found in meadows and occasionally in dry fields or openings in the forest. It may be especially abundant in stands of jewelweed near wet areas. In addition to jewelweed and other plant seeds, the mouse eats grasses, berries, and subterranean fungi. The Meadow Jumping Mouse has only 2 broods annually, with only 3-6 young in each litter. Since this mouse hibernates, it does not have to be as prolific as the rodents that are exposed to predation all year and thus have a higher mortality rate.

Little Brown Bat (not illustrated)

In the fall, the Little Brown Bat acquires a large fat store, finds a cool, moist, communal roost, and falls into *torpor* (a condition where body temperature drops and the heart rate slows). This bat's heart slows to 10-80 beats per minute, the lowest metabolic rate of any mammal. The heart of an active bat beats 600 times per minute. Little Brown Bats may live and reproduce for 30 years. One colony of only 200 Little Brown Bats can eat over 450,000 insects each summer night!

BIRDS

Canada Goose

To Tug Hill residents, the time interval between hearing geese move in spring and in fall seems quite short. Thousands of geese never leave New York State, but instead spend the winter months in local areas where the water stays ice-free. There is a rather extensive movement of geese across the Hill from the Black River Valley to the Lake Ontario Plain in spring and fall.

Red-tailed Hawk

Listen for a shrill, descending scream as this hawk circles above the fields, soaring on thermal air currents. Young birds are covered with white down at first. They spend the day standing on the edge of their nest, waiting for the next meal. Both parents feed their young, and within a few weeks the chicks are as big as adult birds.

American Kestrel (Sparrow Hawk)

The American Kestrel is the smallest and most common member of the Falcon sub-family, and although it can and does kill birds and small mammals, its primary food source is insects such as grasshoppers, dragonflies, and crickets. It is often seen perched on telephone wires, a pole, or fence post watching for prey. The kestrel nests in abandoned woodpecker holes.

Killdeer

The habitat of the Killdeer varies from active cornfields to graveled driveways and parking areas where their eggs may be laid among the stones. Even after a nest is located, it is still difficult to see the eggs because they blend so well with the ground. The young take off running within minutes of hatching. In fall they form very large flocks of up to 200 birds and migrate south.

Ring-billed Gull

Most of the gulls seen on Tug Hill are from the Little Galloo Island colony on Lake Ontario; they make the trip to the Hill daily and return to Little Galloo to roost at night. This gull is an opportunistic feeder and can be seen following a tractor, picking up insect larvae exposed as the soil is turned by the plow. The Ring-billed Gull also catches voles, mice, and snakes that are exposed when hay fields are being cut.

Snowy Owl

The Snowy Owl is a winter visitor and is active during daylight hours. This owl is unafraid of people and will usually tolerate a close enough approach to get a good photograph. Females are larger than males and have more black speckles. The Snowy Owl feeds on rodents and wild pigeons.

Barn Swallow

This is the swallow that you see around a barn where it nests and feeds. The birds dive and swoop all day around the barnyard, fields and meadows feeding on insects. The Barn Swallow builds a mud nest inside a barn or out-building.

Mourning Dove

The name for this bird comes from its mournful song. This dove is a close relative of the extinct Passenger Pigeon that occurred in large numbers on the Hill. Like all members of the family, the young feed on a rich white fluid regurgitated by the adults called *pigeon milk*. The nest of this bird looks like a loose pile of fine sticks on a branch. Mourning Doves do not migrate, though there seems to be some movement off the Hill to the valleys and Lake Ontario Plain, especially to active farms where food supplies are more plentiful. This bird is a Federally regulated game species in most of the states south of New York.

INSECTS AND OTHER INVERTEBRATES

Walking Sticks   (not illustrated)

These insects are so named because they resemble twigs, leaves, and other plant parts. This masquerade gives these docile plant-eaters a measure of protection from hungry predators.

Common Flea

The Common Flea is a very recently evolved and successful insect marvelously adapted as a bloodsucker of vertebrate animals; primarily birds and mammals. The flea is wingless, but possesses amazing jumping ability. It is flattened side-to-side to make moving through its host's feathers or fur easier. Only the adult is a parasite; eggs incubate and larvae live in their host's nests or burrows and feed on nest debris, including their parent's excrement.

Bees   (not illustrated)

Bees are a great benefit to people since they are the primary pollinators of most of our fruit and vegetable plants and most wild plants as well. Most species of bees live solitary lives, but honeybees and bumblebees are colonial. Honeybees were introduced from southern Europe as a source of honey and beeswax, and they have since become part of our wild fauna. Bumblebees nest in the ground and can be quite aggressive around the hive. Carpenter Bees resemble bumblebees, but their abdomens are not hairy and they excavate nest galleries in dead wood, including buildings. Listen for them at work, and look for little piles of sawdust near perfectly round holes in wood.

Wasps and Hornets   (not illustrated)

These insects are stinging insects that may live in a small colony or lead a solitary existence, depending upon the species. A female Paper Wasp will winter under a log or stone and live off stored fat until spring. When she emerges, she is already full of fertilized eggs, having mated the previous fall. She constructs a small nest from a papery material she makes by chewing small bits of wood and mixing it with her saliva. In this nest of several cells suspended by a single stalk, she deposits her first batch of eggs. The hatchling young are sterile workers whose job is to help her construct a larger nest and care for the next brood. The second brood contains some males and new females.

The closely related Bald-faced Hornets and Yellowjackets have a similar life history, but their nest shape and location differs. Both make the same papery material as the Paper Wasp, but a hornet constructs a large conical nest, suspended from a shrub or tree branch. The hornet will defend this nest vigorously, and it will attack in a swarm that drives off most interlopers. The Yellowjacket is an introduced species that usually builds its nest underground or in a tree hole.

A Spider Wasp digs an underground burrow, into which it brings a spider it has paralyzed with the venom in its sting. The helpless spider provides food for the wasp's developing young. The Wolf Spider is the primary prey of the Spider Wasp, and their battles can be fascinating to watch. The wasp attempts to get into a position to sting the spider with its paralyzing venom while the spider struggles to keep its fangs directed towards the wasp. The wasp is usually the victor and it drags the body into an underground tunnel where it lays an egg on the stunned, but still living, spider. The wasp larva eats the spider as it grows and, when mature, emerges from its sealed lair. Watch areas of bare ground to find a wasp digging its tunnel.

Weevils

Weevils are beetles with snouts of various sizes and shapes adapted for feeding on plant juices. Some species are garden pests.

Stink Bug

Although *'bug'* is a name often used to refer to all insects, there is only one group classified by scientists as Bugs. All true bugs possess two pairs of wings held flat across their backs. They all have sucking mouthparts that they use in various ways to obtain food. Leaf Bugs and Stink Bugs suck the juices from living plants. Ambush Bugs and Assassin Bugs capture insects and drain their victims of body fluids. Some, like Bed Bugs, are parasites of birds, mammals, and even people.

Carrion Beetles (not illustrated)

These beetles are commonly found on *carrion* (dead animals). A mated pair will remove the soil from under a dead mouse or other small animal until it is eventually buried. The female deposits her eggs near the mouse, and the developing young feed on the dead flesh.

June Beetles (not illustrated)

This medium-sized beetle is the insect that bounces off your windows in late May and June. It is attracted to lights in your home. The larva, called a grub, may do serious damage to a lawn as it feeds on grass roots.

Ticks and Mites (not illustrated)

Ticks, recognized by their tiny heads, large abdomens, and eight legs are mostly parasitic, feeding on the blood of larger host animals. The tiny Deer Tick transmits Lyme Disease, a serious health threat to people. Mites, as the name suggests, are tiny; some are so small they cannot be seen without the aid of a microscope. They live in a wide variety of habitats, from the tree canopy to forest floor and from deserts to grasslands to wetlands. Some mites are completely aquatic, while others live on the surface of our own bodies. They may be predators, herbivores, scavengers of dead animals or plants, or parasites in and on the bodies of other animals.

Lice (not illustrated)

There are three orders of insects that are commonly referred to as lice, however only one contains species that are parasitic to people. One group, the Booklice, are tiny (one species is the size of the period at the end of this sentence) and are not parasites at all. They live in the leaf litter of the forest floor or under the bark of trees, feeding on plant debris, pollen, and dead insects. Several kinds of lice love the starch-based paste found in older books and can do serious damage to libraries.

The chewing lice are parasites chiefly of birds, feeding on dead skin and feathers. Some species are serious pests of domestic poultry. The sucking lice are blood parasites of mammals, and two species, the Body Louse and the Crab Louse, have evolved so that people are their primary hosts. Both the chewing and sucking lice spend their entire lives on their hosts, including the egg, or *nit*, stage.

Earwigs (not illustrated)

Earwigs are small insects with a peculiar pair of forceps at the back end of their bodies. They get their name from the superstition that they enter people's ears when they are sleeping. They do seek out small crevices in which to hide during the day, which may have given rise to this belief. Some old remedies for ear problems recommend a paste made from pulverized Earwigs be applied to the ear! The most commonly observed species is the European Earwig, an introduced species about ¾ of an inch long and a pest on garden flowers.

Earthworms (not illustrated)

Terrestrial ecosystems simply could not function without earthworms, such as White Worms, Red (or *corn*) Worms, and Nightcrawlers. The cycling of organic nutrients by the worm, and improvement of soil aeration and drainage are extremely important to all growing plants, including agricultural ones.

Photo by Robert McNamara

REFORESTED LANDS

VERIFYING CHARACTERISTICS

- Evergreen Trees of the Same Species
- Trees Planted in Obvious Rows
- No Understory
- Forest Floor Bare Except for Needle Carpet

"There will always be a Tug Hill forest, but the quality of the resource will depend on how it is used and how it is managed today for uses tomorrow"

George Getman

Certain forest types stand out in the landscape because they are dark green, uniform, and have straight edges. A straight line in the landscape is almost always an indicator of the work of people. The extensive areas of reforestation on the Hill are due largely to the Civilian Conservation Corps, or the CCC. The CCC was established during the Depression era to provide jobs by planting trees to control erosion and provide a timber resource. Most of the plantings were softwoods such as Red Pine, White Pine, spruces, and Tamarack.

Walk into the heart of one of these stands and listen. Listen to silence. The dense carpet of needles on the forest floor muffles even your footsteps. Look down the straight rows to the *'windows'* at the ends. Almost nothing can grow through the needle carpet and under the dense shade of the evergreen canopy. Very few native species find the elements of habitat they need to live in these plantations.

The plantations were planted at a time when it was thought that forest resources could be managed in a monoculture, like croplands. Modern practices on the Hill today are more comprehensive, managing not only for timber resources but also wildlife, forest recreation, and visual resources. Selective logging, timber stand improvement measures, natural regeneration, and other methods are more often employed for multi-use management.

ILLUSTRATIONS

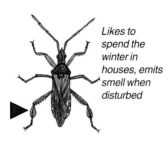

Likes to spend the winter in houses, emits smell when disturbed

Western Conifer Seed Bug
Length to 1"

Scissor bill

Red Crossbill
Length 6 1/4"

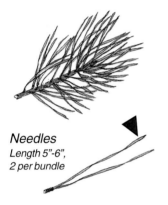

Needles
*Length 5"-6",
2 per bundle*

Bark
*Deep ridges
covered with
flaky scales*

Cone
*Length
2"-2 1/4"*

Red Pine
Max. height 100', common 70'-80'

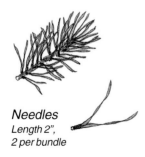

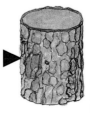

Bark
*Bark on trunk
scaly, upper trunk
& limbs orange*

Cone
*Length
1"-3"*

Needles
*Length 2",
2 per bundle*

Scotch Pine
Max. height 100', common 40'-60'

FACTS, TIPS, AND LORE

FACTS, TIPS, *AND* LORE
REFORESTED LANDS

BIRDS

Red Crossbill

The upper and lower mandibles of this bird are not aligned, hence the name crossbill. This is a special adaptation employed to pry cones open to get at the seeds. This bird is nomadic and nests where cone crops are high. The Red Crossbill nests in the dead of winter, as early as January or February. Watch for a flock of Red Crossbills in the road in winter feeding on road salt.

PART THREE
LOWLANDS

WOODED SWAMPS

VERIFYING CHARACTERISTICS

- Trees Growing in Hummocky, Often Saturated Low Areas
- Low Areas Dominated by a Single Tree Species, Whether Hardwood or Softwood.
- Generally Level Terrain

"As we advance to the Salmon river, we find land fit for settlers; some good swales and very little hemlock"

From the journal of James Constable

Several tree species can grow with *'wet feet'*; they can tolerate flooded roots for an extended period of time. There are many low lying, flat places on the Hill; in the backwaters of beaver flows, in the floodplains of creeks and rivers, and as transitional zones between many lowlands and uplands. One or more of the water tolerant species of trees colonize these wet areas: **Red Maple (Soft Maple), Eastern Hemlock, Tamarack (Larch)**, and Balsam Fir, depending upon subtle differences in soil type and climate. Balsam Fir is one of the most obvious representatives of the northern forest of the Adirondacks and Canada that occupies the Tug Hill transitional plant communities. In southern areas of the Hill, Eastern Hemlock is the predominant evergreen species in the wooded swamps. Walk beneath the dense hemlock canopy and you can feel the shelter that is so important to wintering deer. The shade is so dense that almost nothing grows on the hemlock forest floor. Several species of animals and birds take advantage of the fact that wooded swamps can be difficult places to walk through and use this habitat for shelter.

Spring

Where beaver flows meet wooded swamps there is often a zone of standing dead trees with bleached trunks that died when the water table was elevated by beaver activity. Look for numerous platforms of sticks wedged into the crotches of these trees. They are nests of the Great Blue Heron, a bird that is a *colonial nester* (the nests of many mating pairs that are built in close proximity). The seclusion and protection offered by the watery moat and the openness of the barren trunks that denies cover to predators makes these areas ideal for heron rookeries. If you find one, use your binoculars to watch from a distance so you will not disturb the nesters.

Summer

It is usually late summer before you can walk in the swamp without getting wet, and when the biting insects have tapered off enough to make the visit tolerable. This is the time when the understory of ferns and herbaceous plants has grown to a staggering density. Stands of **Royal Fern** can reach head height. Stand quietly next to a tree and listen for the tapping and prying sounds of woodpeckers picking over the many dead limbs and trunks.

Fall

The golden fall color of the Tamarack is the best clue for identifying this unique tree. The Tamarack is a *deciduous softwood* (it drops its needles in the fall). Look for a golden ring around a bog or wet meadow in fall. Other wooded swamps are ringed with scarlet as early as late August, when the Red Maples start to turn.

Winter

Winter is the best time to explore the swamps without getting soaked and covered with *sticktights* (seeds that cling to animals and people for dispersal). Even in winter many plants can be identified by studying dried seed heads, plant form, and other clues. The variety and complexity of seed structures is fascinating, and the methods of dispersal ingenious.

White-tailed Deer often choose a dense hemlock swamp for their winter yard because of the shelter it offers and the lack of snow beneath the interlocking tree crowns. When snow piles up on the evergreens, much of it evaporates or melts before it hits the ground, so there is less snow under evergreen trees than there is on the ground under hardwood trees in the same region. Evergreens with branches close to the ground also reduce wind and cold airflow, and help the deer reduce heat loss.

ILLUSTRATIONS

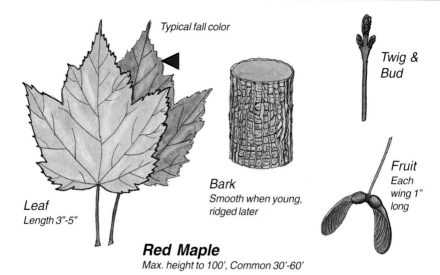

Typical fall color

Twig & Bud

Bark
Smooth when young, ridged later

Fruit
Each wing 1" long

Leaf
Length 3"-5"

Red Maple
Max. height to 100', Common 30'-60'

Needles
Length 1/2"-2/3", two parallel lines on lower surface, round tipped

Bark
Uniform ridges

Cone
Length 1/2"-3/4"

Eastern Hemlock
Height 50'-80'

Needles
Length 3/4"-1 1/4", deciduous, triangular in cross-section

Bark
Deep ridges made of flaky scales, reddish-brown beneath scales

Cone
Length 1/2"-3/4"

Tamarack
Height 40'-80'

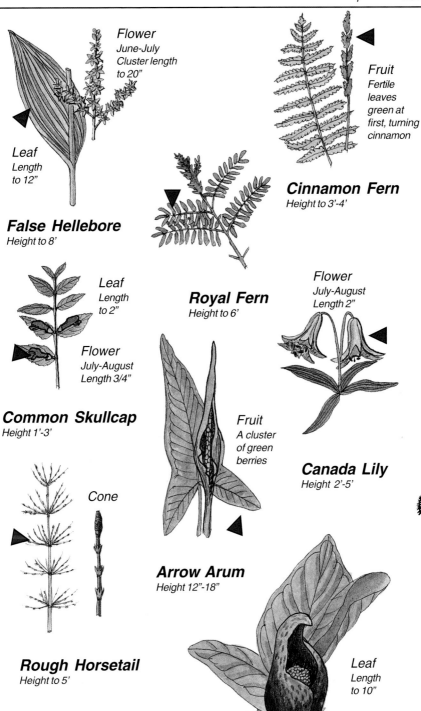

Flower
June-July
Cluster length
to 20"

Leaf
Length
to 12"

False Hellebore
Height to 8'

Fruit
Fertile
leaves
green at
first, turning
cinnamon

Cinnamon Fern
Height to 3'-4'

Royal Fern
Height to 6'

Leaf
Length
to 2"

Flower
July-August
Length 3/4"

Common Skullcap
Height 1'-3'

Flower
July-August
Length 2"

Fruit
A cluster
of green
berries

Canada Lily
Height 2'-5'

Cone

Rough Horsetail
Height to 5'

Arrow Arum
Height 12"-18"

Leaf
Length
to 10"

Skunk Cabbage
Height 1'-3', fetid odor

FACTS, TIPS, AND LORE

FACTS, TIPS, AND LORE
WOODED SWAMPS

TREES

Red Maple (Soft Maple)

This tree is red in spring because it is covered with red flowers that appear before the leaves, and its leaves turn red in the fall. The tree is called *Soft Maple* because its wood is not as dense and durable as Sugar Maple (Hard Maple). This tree also grows on upland sites. Historically the tree was used for production of sulfuric acid.

Eastern Hemlock

This evergreen is extremely shade tolerant, and grows in the deepest shadows of the forest. It is usually found in homogenous stands in low areas or scattered along the edge of a stream or swamp. Its bark was once used as a source of tannin for tanning hides, and the wood was sometimes discarded. Now it is used widely as rough lumber for building construction.

Tamarack (Larch)

The Tamarack is most obvious in October when it turns a bright gold and drops its needles. The wood is resistant to decay but difficult to work because of the great difference in hardness between the spring and summer portions of the growth rings.

HERBACEOUS PLANTS

False Hellebore

This plant is one of the first green plants to poke through the surface as the snow melts, and is often confused with Skunk Cabbage. A close look reveals very different leaf and flower structures and in a short time this plant grows to head height, while the true Skunk Cabbage stays close to the ground. WARNING: False Hellebore is very poisonous if eaten.

FERNS

Cinnamon Fern

Cinnamon Fern is a large fern that forms hummocky thickets in wet areas. Cinnamon colored fertile leaflets grow on separate stalks, giving this fern its name. Also look for cinnamon colored woolly tufts at the base of the sterile leaflets. These persistent tufts help identify the fern, even in winter.

Royal Fern

This is a large fern with leaves that have rows of leaf stalks on both sides of the main rib, which in turn have rows of leaflets. It grows in wet spots in fallow fields and other wet areas.

Rough Horsetail (Scouring Rush)

This plant is called Scouring Rush because its stem contains silica, and the plant was once used as a pot scrubber. Like the clubmosses, horsetails are *fern-allies* (plants that are closely related to ferns).

Three-lobed Bazzania (not illustrated)

This plant is a leafy liverwort and looks like a robust, dark green moss. It is a primitive-looking plant that grows on decaying logs and stumps. Its leaves overlap like shingles on a roof.

 MAMMALS

Virginia Opossum   (not illustrated)

Playing 'possum' is a defense mechanism for which this animal is well known. When threatened by a predator it lapses into a catatonic state, and it is thought that its lack of movement as well as its bad smell causes the predator to lose interest. The 'possum is a very adaptable animal and it will eat almost anything. It is the only *marsupial* (the female has a pouch) in the United States. Newborn young, 1/2 inch long and weighing less than a penny pull themselves along their mother's fur to her pouch where they attach to a nipple and continue their development. The 'possum has been steadily extending its range northward. It has only been in the last 20 years that this creature has occupied Tug Hill.

Photo by Robert McNamara

MARSHES *and* WET MEADOWS

VERIFYING CHARACTERISTICS

- Standing Water Between Hummocks
  of Vegetation
- Rotten Egg Smell when Disturbed

*"The spring peeper is clearly one of the most common
vertebrate animals on Tug Hill...nearly everyone has heard
the peep...yet few people have seen one."*

Glenn Johnson

Would you wade through knee deep water, mucky ooze sucking at
your shoes, methane gas wafting up from the surface, brushing aside
spider webs, and swatting at clouds of mosquitoes? Probably not by
choice. The seclusion and protection offered to wildlife by the marsh
is one of its greatest values, but there is much to see in the marsh if you
can overcome a few obstacles and protect yourself from insects.

The transition zone from wetland to upland is a good place to catch
some action, and it is the easiest place to walk without sinking in the
muck. Put on your boots and take a closer look at those swampy areas
that often seem to be a nuisance. There are many different types of
wetlands that have been described by scientists based on the plant
communities present and the soil and water characteristics. A
wetland with cattails is a *deep emergent marsh,* and a bog could be
a *rich graminoid (grassy) fen.* On Tug Hill, many people lump them
all together and label them swamps, often with a derogatory tone.

It was once thought that wet areas had no value until drained or filled
and converted to pasture, cropland, or building sites. Only in recent
years have people begun to appreciate the importance of the functions
of wetlands in a healthy ecosystem. Wetlands provide flood control,
aquifer recharge, and they are a highly productive wildlife habitat.
Wetlands are full of fascinating creatures and are critical to certain stages

in the life cycles of many species that you usually find on dry ground.

At first glance the grass-like plants that grow in wet meadows all look alike, but if you look closely you will see that they are indeed different. Most grasses have *nodes* or *joints* (swollen places on the stem at the leaf joints) and round, hollow stems. If you gently pull the leaf away from the stem, the base (called the sheath) opens up rather than tears. Sedges do not have nodes, and if you pull the leaf away from the stem of a sedge, the sheath tears. Easiest to remember, though, is that *'sedges have edges'*, referring to the stems that are triangular in cross section and solid. Rushes are a smaller group of plants compared to grasses and sedges. The small flowers of rushes have three petals, three sepals, and look like a lily.

Grasses are of enormous economic importance; they provide most of the major food sources of the world. Wheat, Barley, Oats, Corn, Rye, Rice, Millet, and Sorghum are grasses. In our area they are important agricultural plants for pasture and hay, and are the major component of abandoned agricultural fields. The value of sedges has never equaled the economic importance of grasses. Most sedges are inedible, and they typically grow in colder and wetter areas than grasses. Rushes, like sedges, also typically grow in cold and wet areas and though they are not economically important, chair caners know them as the material they use for caned seats.

Spring

The marsh offers a three-season program of musical entertainment. In the spring, when ice is still lingering, the first Wood Frogs start to chorus, soon joined by **Spring Peepers**, then followed by a progression of frog species that lasts well into summer.

Go out in the evening with your flashlight (used sparingly) and look into the water and along the edges of the marsh. At times the water is teeming with mating frogs. Tiny Spring Peeper males gather in the weedy vegetation at the edge of ponds to call females for mating. After mating, the female attaches eggs individually to underwater plants, and the eggs hatch within a week. After about 45-60 days, depending partly on water temperature, the developed tadpoles emerge from the water and crawl out into the leafy litter of the forest floor.

Listen for the long, musical trill of the **American Toad** beginning early in April. The song, made by a male advertising for a mate, can be

Tug Hill Frog Song Schedule

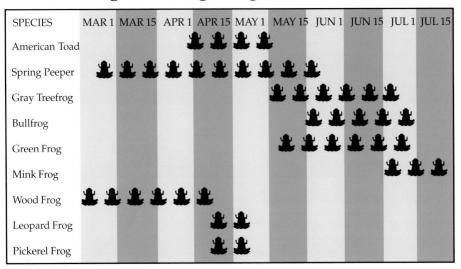

SPECIES	MAR 1	MAR 15	APR 1	APR 15	MAY 1	MAY 15	JUN 1	JUN 15	JUL 1	JUL 15
American Toad			🐸	🐸	🐸	🐸				
Spring Peeper	🐸	🐸	🐸	🐸	🐸	🐸	🐸	🐸	🐸	
Gray Treefrog						🐸	🐸	🐸	🐸	🐸
Bullfrog							🐸	🐸	🐸	🐸
Green Frog							🐸	🐸	🐸	🐸
Mink Frog									🐸	🐸
Wood Frog	🐸	🐸	🐸	🐸	🐸	🐸				
Leopard Frog					🐸	🐸				
Pickerel Frog					🐸	🐸				

imitated by whistling and humming at the same time. The coarse dry skin of the American Toad allows it to spend most of its life on land, but it comes to the marsh, or almost any other wet area in spring, to sing and deposit strings of eggs. Shine your light across the surface of the water and look for a toad with an inflated throat pouch singing from a patch of duckweed or algae.

Turn off the light and, if the time is right, you may see stars on the ground and stars overhead at the same time. The tiny points of light coming from banks along the edge of some wet areas are *Glowworms*, the larval form of the Lightning Bug.

No matter how still and quiet you are, it is difficult to escape detection by the **Great Blue Heron**. While quite tame along large lakes, a heron on the Hill usually takes flight before you can get within 100 yards of it. If you surprise a heron while sneaking up to a pond you will probably hear its harsh guttural *'squawk'* as it flies up and lands again a safe distance away. Only by getting close can you appreciate the size of the bird; it is nearly 4 feet tall with a wingspan of more than 6 feet. Watching a heron hunt is a treat worth a little patience. Although awkward-looking in flight, a heron is stealthy, graceful, and lightning quick when hunting. The Great Blue Heron is often called a *crane* by Hill residents, but there are no true cranes native to Tug Hill.

One of the first birds to be heard in spring is the male **Red-winged Blackbird**. If you live near a marsh, he is as much a harbinger of spring as is the robin. The male returns first, stakes out a territory, and calls to attract a female. The bright red shoulder patch, or *epaulet*, of the male is clearly visible as he calls and stretches his wings to flash the bright color that advertises his presence.

No matter what time of day or night, spring is a great time to explore the marsh. Starting in May, the marsh becomes the domain of the biting flies and the air sings with the whine of thousands of wings. The *mosquito* is the most conspicuous of the pesky insects. The female mosquito lays her eggs directly in the

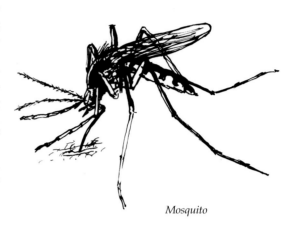

Mosquito

water. It is easy to find the larvae of mosquitoes, called *wrigglers*, in almost any puddle. The female mosquito is the biter; she uses her specialized piercing mouthparts to suck blood from our bodies. The anticoagulants in her saliva are responsible for the itching of a mosquito bite. The male mosquito either feeds on flower nectar or does not feed at all. Few insects have had more of an impact on people than mosquitoes, but any attempt to eradicate them is not a wise management strategy. The mosquito is an important food source for nesting birds and other insects. It is best to protect yourself from attack with the proper clothing and repellents.

Summer

On an early summer evening the marsh seems to vibrate with a low frequency 'jug-o-rum' chorus. The **Bullfrog** makes this sound and is familiar to those who like froglegs. With practice they can be approached for a close look. Those just learning the skill will hear a loud splash like a log hitting the water before they ever see the frog. Move slowly along the edge and watch ahead for frogs. At first you will probably hear a chirp and a splash and see only ripples, but with some practice you will see many species of frogs before they leap.

You may hear a different call mixed in with the Bullfrog chorus that sounds like the plucking of a banjo string. The Green Frog, one of the most common mid-sized Tug Hill frogs, makes this call. The male Green Frog, like the Bullfrog, has a large eardrum that is bigger in diameter than its eye. The eardrum of the female is smaller than her eye. Like most frogs, the Green Frog is a visual predator and will react by orienting its body toward any small movement around it. If you look closely as a frog catches an insect, it seems like it closes its eyes as it swallows. This happens because the muscles that pull food towards the back of the frog's throat and push it down into the frog's stomach are attached to the eyeball. By mid-summer the frogs quiet down and the collective voices of countless insects change the chorus to buzzes, chirps, and whistles.

Fall

It seems that before summer has even completely arrived, the first signs of fall are starting to appear. Grasses, sedges, and herbaceous plants have gone to seed and are distributing their seeds in various ingenious ways. Cottony **Swamp Milkweed** strands float through the air. Migrating birds eat and deposit ripened berries. Brush against a **Spotted Jewelweed** and get a big surprise. The seedpods explode on contact, throwing seeds in all directions. To examine the contents of the pod, gently pluck one without touching it and then close your fist on it to contain the explosion. You will see the springing mechanism; a coiled, wiry strand that is bound tightly inside with the seeds. Spotted Jewelweed is found in extensive beds in wet areas with woodland shade. The plant is called jewelweed because a leaf submerged in water has a silvery look caused by air held within nearly invisible hairs on its surface. The flowers are an important food source for butterflies, bumblebees, wild honeybees, and hummingbirds. Deer heavily browse the stems and leaves in summer months.

By late August, the first red leaves of Gray Dogwood and Red Maple appear in and along the edges of the wet meadows. By September, migratory birds have fledged their young and are feeding on the abundant seed crops, the late nectars, and insect hatches in an effort to store the energy reserves they will need for the long flight south. Breeding plumages have been replaced by the fall molt, making birds like the warblers even more of a challenge to identify.

An important avian predator of the marsh is the **Northern Harrier** or *Marsh Hawk*. This raptor breeds on Tug Hill and usually nests in wet meadows. Look for the harrier as it methodically courses low over the marsh. This predator tips its wings from side to side as it searches for prey across the marsh, then it changes course and scans another line, systematically covering every inch of territory.

Watch the open water of the marsh for the frenzied activity of the **Muskrat**. Look for a small, mound-shaped hut of cattails and other aquatic plants that looks like a miniature version of a beaver lodge. This house of vegetation provides a dry nest and a stable temperature within. The house may be up to 8 feet in diameter and 4 feet tall, with 1 foot thick walls. Chambers are created within, with several plunge holes that allow the inhabitants to escape directly into the water if necessary. Smaller mounds, circular like the main hut but only about 1 foot above water level, are for feeding and do not have internal chambers.

The Muskrat lives along a bank, ditch, or shoreline and it will often make a burrow system in the bank. This burrow system may be very complex; the openings are 4-5 inches in diameter, and the burrows may extend up to 45 feet from the entrance. Tunnel entrances are usually below water level and surface openings are plugged with vegetation, especially when the *'rat'* is at home.

Muskrat huts are good places to watch for other animals. Snapping Turtles lay their eggs in these structures, toads and snakes may live within the houses and even winter there, and many animals use the structures as basking spots. The huts and mounds, dry islands in a sea of productive marsh, may also be used as nesting sites by Canada Geese, ducks, and other birds.

Winter

When the cold weather arrives, the symphony ends and the marsh falls silent. The music makers have migrated, hibernated, or *metamorphosed* (changed form) for winter. Winter is the time to put on the snowshoes and explore the marsh from a perspective that is hard to attain any other time of the year. Be careful of weak ice and soft spots, especially near vegetation, as the heat generated by plant decomposition fights the formation of solid ice in places. Discover where the Red-winged Blackbird and Common Yellowthroat nested. The seedpods left behind by the marsh plants are often the best clues for identification.

The Muskrat creates *'pushups'* in winter; these loose piles of vegetation and roots are pushed up through a breathing hole in the ice to keep the hole open and allow the *'rat'* to safely surface for air following feeding dives. Pushups are temporary, and sink into the water as the ice melts.

Wood Turtle

ILLUSTRATIONS

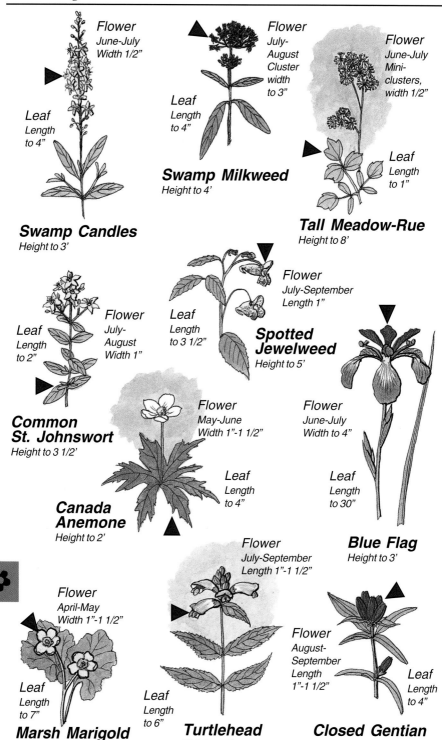

Flower
June-July
Width 1/2"

Leaf
Length
to 4"

Swamp Candles
Height to 3'

Flower
July-
August
Cluster
width
to 3"

Leaf
Length
to 4"

Swamp Milkweed
Height to 4'

Flower
June-July
Mini-
clusters,
width 1/2"

Leaf
Length
to 1"

Tall Meadow-Rue
Height to 8'

Flower
July-
August
Width 1"

Leaf
Length
to 2"

**Common
St. Johnswort**
Height to 3 1/2'

Leaf
Length
to 3 1/2"

Flower
July-September
Length 1"

**Spotted
Jewelweed**
Height to 5'

Flower
June-July
Width to 4"

Leaf
Length
to 30"

Blue Flag
Height to 3'

Flower
May-June
Width 1"-1 1/2"

Leaf
Length
to 4"

**Canada
Anemone**
Height to 2'

Flower
April-May
Width 1"-1 1/2"

Leaf
Length
to 7"

Marsh Marigold
Height to 2'

Flower
July-September
Length 1"-1 1/2"

Leaf
Length
to 6"

Turtlehead
Height to 3'

Flower
August-
September
Length
1"-1 1/2"

Leaf
Length
to 4"

Closed Gentian
Height to 2'

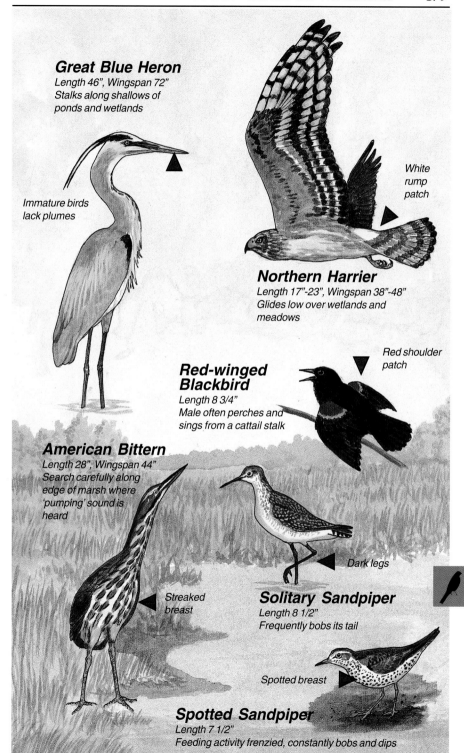

Great Blue Heron
Length 46", Wingspan 72"
Stalks along shallows of
ponds and wetlands

Immature birds
lack plumes

White
rump
patch

Northern Harrier
Length 17"-23", Wingspan 38"-48"
Glides low over wetlands and
meadows

Red shoulder
patch

Red-winged
Blackbird
Length 8 3/4"
Male often perches and
sings from a cattail stalk

American Bittern
Length 28", Wingspan 44"
Search carefully along
edge of marsh where
'pumping' sound is
heard

Dark legs

Streaked
breast

Solitary Sandpiper
Length 8 1/2"
Frequently bobs its tail

Spotted breast

Spotted Sandpiper
Length 7 1/2"
Feeding activity frenzied, constantly bobs and dips

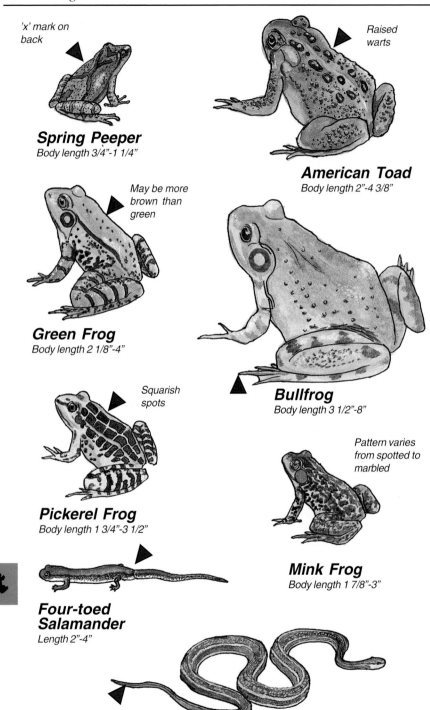

'x' mark on back

Spring Peeper
Body length 3/4"-1 1/4"

Raised warts

American Toad
Body length 2"-4 3/8"

May be more brown than green

Green Frog
Body length 2 1/8"-4"

Bullfrog
Body length 3 1/2"-8"

Squarish spots

Pickerel Frog
Body length 1 3/4"-3 1/2"

Pattern varies from spotted to marbled

Mink Frog
Body length 1 7/8"-3"

Four-toed Salamander
Length 2"-4"

Eastern Ribbon Snake
Length 18"-40"

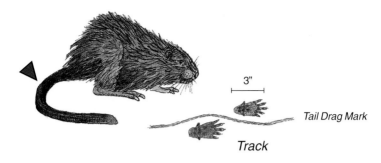

Tail Drag Mark

Track

Muskrat
Body 10"-14", tail 10"-12"

Harvester
Wingspan 1 1/8"-1 1/4"

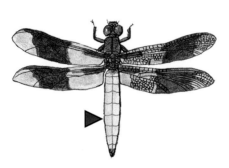

White Tail Dragonfly
Wingspan 2 1/2"-3"

Red Admiral
Wingspan 2 1/4"-3"

Predacious Diving Beetle
Length to 1 1/4"

Whirligig Beetle
Length 3/8"-5/8"

FACTS, TIPS, AND LORE

FACTS, TIPS, AND LORE
MARSHES AND WET MEADOWS

SHRUBS

Winterberry   (not illustrated)

Winterberry is a northern representative of the holly family. It has red berries, but they are the only typical holly feature. Unlike the spiny, thick evergreen leaves of the southern hollys, this shrub is deciduous and the leaves are not spiny. This is the shrub that stands out in the winter marsh because of the showy clusters of bright red berries. Winterberry fruit is attractive to birds, and the fruit is persistent enough to serve as a food source for spring migrants.

Black Huckleberry   (not illustrated)

Black Huckleberry, one of several varieties of huckleberries, is a favorite of people and many species of birds and mammals. The berries are similar to the blueberries, but these berries do not usually have the dusty whitish coating.

Sheep Laurel   (not illustrated)

The showy flowers of the Sheep Laurel are unique among the several shrubs found in the thickets bordering and scattered throughout the marsh. Look closely at the stamens and note how they are tucked into the petals. They release when touched, providing a mechanism for attaching pollen to nectar eaters. This plant is avoided by livestock and thought to be poisonous.

Leatherleaf   (not illustrated)

This shrub is named for its leathery leaves that persist into winter. Individual plants are difficult to distinguish since they grow in clusters, with multiple stems that slant out toward the open marsh.

HERBACEOUS PLANTS

Spotted Jewelweed, Pale Jewelweed   (not illustrated)

There are two common species of jewelweed, Spotted Jewelweed with orange to yellow flowers about 1 inch in size and Pale Jewelweed with larger, 1 1/2 inch, pale yellow flowers. Both have translucent stems that contain mucilaginous juices said to relieve itching from poison ivy and athlete's foot.

Turtlehead

Turtlehead was named for the swollen, two-lipped white flowers that resemble the head of a turtle. There is a variety of the plant that has red flowers, and as the white flowers age they also turn a reddish color. This plant grows in wet areas and streamsides, and it is the principal food plant for the Baltimore Butterfly Caterpillar. Historically, Turtlehead was used as a folk remedy for fever, jaundice, worms, and as a laxative.

Closed Gentian (Bottle Gentian)

This perennial plant grows in wet meadows and moist thickets, and sometimes grows in profusion where the land has been disturbed.

Smartweed   (Lady's Thumb) (not illustrated)

A marsh covered with the flowering Smartweed is a dazzling display of red color. The seeds are small and prolific, and grow in tight clusters around the stem. They are important as a source of food for waterfowl and furbearers. WARNING: The fresh juice is acrid and may cause skin irritation in sensitive people.

Marsh Marigold (Cowslip)

The bright yellow flowers of Marsh Marigold bring a cheery note to a dreary landscape in early spring. The young leaves and flowers should not be eaten raw as they contain a poison that causes violent gastritis and is toxic to the heart. The juice from the plant may also irritate skin. WARNING: Poisonous

Blue Flag

With its sword shaped leaves and large, brilliant blue flowers, this Iris is sure to be noticed. The name *'Iris'* is in honor of the Greek goddess of the rainbow. The yellow lines and dark veins on the flower petals guide bees, the primary pollinator, to the nectar. When in bloom, an iris patch is also a great place to see hummingbirds. Native Americans planted Blue Flag near their villages to harvest for medicinal uses. The *rhizomes* (underground root-like stems) of Blue Flag are poisonous.

Wild Mint   (not illustrated)

The signature of this plant is its minty smell. It is used for tea or garnish, and medicinally for stomach gas. Other introduced species of mint have spread from gardens into the wild. Most are edible except for one, Pennyroyal, which should not be taken internally.

Sweet-scented Water Lily   (not illustrated)

Look into the showy, fragrant white Water Lily flower to see the beautiful and complex structure that looks like a wax sculpture. The floating platforms and underwater parts of the plant shelter frogs and many insects. Fishermen use the plants as an indicator of water depth, since they usually grow in water 2-4 feet deep.

GRASS-LIKE PLANTS

Cattail   (not illustrated)

This familiar herbaceous plant is grass-like, but is actually not a grass, sedge, or rush. This plant is a major component of marsh habitats and it provides food and shelter for many animals. Muskrats use the stalks to build their lodges and they eat the roots. Many parts of the Cattail are also edible and useful to people, earning it the name *'supermarket of the wild'* from the late Euell Gibbons, a celebrated edible plant specialist. The alien Purple Loosestrife threatens cattail marshes.

Reed Canary Grass   (not illustrated)

The branched *inflorescence* (flower cluster) of Reed Canary Grass is open when it is in flower, then it closes. This is a 3-4 foot tall colonial grass that spreads by *rhizomes* (underground stems that send out roots and shoots). Settlers discovered that it makes good hay.

Rattlesnake Grass, Fowl Manna Grass   (not illustrated)

Rattlesnake Grass is a fairly tall (to about 3 feet) grass of wet places. The non-flowering stems of Rattlesnake Grass and the related Fowl Manna Grass look a bit like palm fronds in that the leaves branch off the stem somewhat like a palm. Fowl Manna Grass has smaller flower clusters than Rattlesnake Grass and they tend to be purple tinged, whereas the flower clusters of Rattlesnake Grass are green. Both flower in spring, and the flower clusters disintegrate by late summer.

Tussock Sedge   (not illustrated)

This sedge is usually found in large populations and can readily be recognized by the numerous tussocks. These tussocks are often 1- 2 feet above the wet muck, and it is sorely tempting to traverse a marsh by tussock hopping. However, it is very likely you will fall off an unstable tussock. The tussocks provide nesting cover for some marsh birds, and the seeds of Tussock Sedge, and other sedges, are eaten by many birds.

Soft Rush   (not illustrated)

The most common rush that you will encounter on Tug Hill is Soft Rush. Look closely at the small, lily-like flower for 6 petals (actually 3 petals and 3 sepals, but since they are virtually indistinguishable, they are called *tepals*). Soft Rush tends to grow in clumps, though it does not form tussocks. If you open the small fruit, you will see many small seeds.

 FERNS

Sensitive Fern   (not illustrated)

The fronds of this fern turn brown and wither with the slightest frost, giving the plant its name. The beaded fertile fronds persist through winter and are an easy clue to identification.

MAMMALS

Muskrat

The Muskrat is often nocturnal, although the best chance to see one during the day is in spring and early summer. The animal gets its name from a musky odor that it deposits throughout its territory during the breeding season. Muskrats eat Cattail, Burreed, Bulrush, Arrowhead, sedges, Duckweed and Pondweed, Pickerelweed, grasses, and they will even eat clams, carp, snails, and crayfish.

BIRDS

American Bittern

The camouflaged coloration and habit of *'freezing'*, pointing its head and neck straight up when threatened, makes this bird nearly impossible to spot. Listen for a pumping sound coming from the cattails, *'oonck-a-tsoonck, oonck-a-tsoonck'*. This bird is an uncommon species that has declined in the last 20 years, even in prime habitat areas. The bittern needs extensive marshlands for feeding and nesting. This bird feeds on fish, frogs, salamanders, and some larger insect larvae. The bittern sits motionless along the marsh edge and lets the food come to it, rather than walking along the edge as does its close relative, the heron.

Northern Harrier

The official common name of this bird of prey was changed from Marsh Hawk to Northern Harrier. The harrier hunts for birds, small mammals, snakes, and frogs over wetlands and wet woods. Its facial disks help it pick up the sounds of prey animals as they move through the vegetation. The female is about one third larger than the male. When the male brings prey for a female on the nest, she flies up to greet him. He often drops the food before the transfer is complete and she pursues it and catches it in mid-air.

Great Blue Heron

Watch a heron feed from a hidden spot and you will notice that after it catches a fish the bird will shake it to stun it, then position it with the head down to be swallowed whole. Watch the bulge in its neck as the fish travels down.

Green Heron   (not illustrated)

This small heron is less conspicuous than the Great Blue Heron, but no less showy. You have to get close to appreciate the colors of its plumage. Watch the marsh any time of day in June and you should see this bird stalking the shallows, catching frogs and insects to feed its nestlings.

Solitary Sandpiper, Spotted Sandpiper

These are two of several species of predominantly brown birds that feed along the edges of open water, known collectively as Shorebirds. Watch the habits of these birds as they feed and fly. Each species is adapted for a particular section of the edge, some having long legs and bills, others short legged and with small bills. These adaptations allow the birds to coexist without competing for the same food supply. Distinguishing between species takes patient study and a good pair of binoculars.

Red-winged Blackbird

A chorus of blackbird songs echoes over every marsh in spring. Each male bird stakes out a portion of the marsh as his and defends it aggressively. The females arrive later and mating and nesting begins. In fall these birds gather together in great flocks before migration. Standing in the middle of one of these flocks as it flows through the trees is exciting and must have been the inspiration for the Hitchcock movie 'The Birds'.

AMPHIBIANS and REPTILES

Four-toed Salamander

A distinguishing feature of this small salamander is the conspicuous constriction at the base of the tail. A common defense it employs is to present its tail to a would-be attacker such as a bird or snake. The predator grabs the tail, which promptly breaks off at the constriction. The tail keeps wriggling and occupies the predator's attention while the rest of the salamander scurries to cover. The tail will eventually grow back.

American Toad

This toad is most often seen scurrying from underfoot as you walk along on moist ground. Notice the pair of large, bean-shaped glands located just behind the head. These glands produce a mild poison that the toad stores in its bladder. When handled, the toad will produce copious amounts of urine with enough of this foul-tasting toxin to deter most predators. As a consequence, the toad does not have to be a good jumper to escape its enemies.

Bullfrog

The Bullfrog is the clear winner in the size department among Tug Hill frogs, attaining a length of up to 8″ from snout to tailbone. Like all amphibians, the Bullfrog is carnivorous and will attempt to eat any animal that will fit into its considerable mouth, including insects, snakes, other frogs, and even birds and mammals. The male Bullfrog establishes a territory at the edge of the water in late spring and defends it against all comers. Several small males may hide in vegetation at the edge of a large male's territory. They do not advertise their presence by calling because the larger male will eat them if discovered. Known as satellite males, these individuals attempt to intercept and mate with females attracted by the call of the larger male. Their success rate is low, however.

Mink Frog

The Mink Frog may be found in the colder waters of Tug Hill uplands. It is similar to the Green Frog. Careful examination of the spotting pattern across the folded hind limbs reveals a random pattern on Mink Frogs and a continuous pattern on Green Frogs. The presence of a strong musky odor on your hands after you release one will clinch the identification as a Mink Frog.

Pickerel Frog

The Pickerel Frog is found of the grassy and weedy borders of ponds, and is often quite a distance from the water. Its early spring staccato call sounds like a loud snore.

Spotted Turtle   (not illustrated)

This turtle retreats to muskrat burrows and tangled mats of vegetation and lies dormant during the hot summer months. Unlike other turtles, the Spotted Turtle takes great care with its nest. The turtle carefully places 3-4 the eggs in a nest dug out in loose ground, uses its hind feet to cover them with soil, and then smoothes the surface. Despite this attention, a Raccoon or skunk will often discover the nest.

Wood Turtle

This turtle spends a great deal of time on land and possesses an intelligence un-characteristic of turtles. It can learn to run a simple maze, and it has been observed stomping the earth to scare up earthworms, one of its prey species. The Wood Turtle also eats aquatic insects, snails, and crayfish.

Eastern Painted Turtle   (not illustrated)

Carefully scan logs and tree stumps protruding from the surface of open water and you may see Painted Turtles basking in the sun. If few logs are available, large groups of these turtles will share the same space. They are extremely wary and will drop into the water in the blink of an eye. A mature male can be readily distinguished from a female by its very long front claws. It uses the claws to stroke the cheeks of the female in an effort to court and successfully mate with her.

Eastern Ribbon Snake

Look for this snake along the edge of open water areas in the marsh. It may be easily found in certain marshes, but overall it is quite uncommon. It feeds primarily on fish, frogs and tadpoles, and like its relative the Garter Snake, gives birth to living young.

INSECTS

Red Admiral (Banded Orange)

Look for this butterfly basking in full sunlight on a road or trail where a male will protect his selected territory and drive off intruders. Look for the caterpillar feeding on Nettle, False Nettle, Wood Nettle, and possibly Wild Hops. The Red Admiral is a regular migrant that must re-colonize the coldest portions of the north each year.

Harvester (The Wanderer)

The larva of this butterfly is a predator of aphids and other unarmored scale insects that live on alders. Not only does the larva feed on the aphids, but lives within the white downy aphid mass you often see on the branches of alders. Why the aphids do not recognize it as a predator is not fully understood. Look for adults around alder beds near slowstreams.

White Tail Dragonfly

The male White Tail Dragonfly is often seen resting with its head down and abdomen raised, with its wings forward and drooping. It is likely to be seen resting near water or flying over small pools in the marsh. Look for a group of resting white tails on a branch or log just out of the water.

Whirligig Beetle

This diving beetle can be seen swirling in a group on the surface film of still water. It is well adapted for swimming, with a flattened, smooth body, paddle shaped hind legs fringed with hairs, and divided eyes; one looking up from the water surface and one looking down. When this beetle dives it carries a bubble of water with it as a source of oxygen.

Fall Reflections - Beaver

Painting by Robert McNamara

BEAVER FLOWS AND CREEKS

VERIFYING CHARACTERISTICS

- Flowing, Clear Water
- Flooded Trees
- Freshly Chewed Stumps

*"Beaver dams cause ponds to develop along
a watercourse that look, from above,
like a string of pearls."*

Lee B. Chamberlaine

The **Beaver** is not the favorite animal of many highway superintendents, loggers, or farmers. The activities of Beaver often conflict with the industries of people. It is true that the Beaver plugs culverts and floods woodlots and fields, but try to look at its labors in a different way. A stream that has an active Beaver population constantly changes in a repeating cycle from open water to shrub covered meadow. Beaver dams cause ponds to develop along a watercourse that look, from above, like a string of pearls. A given watercourse will be dotted with flows of different ages. The diversity of habitat types thus created along the streams supports a tremendous diversity of species from algae to mammals. A stream with Beaver activity is the best habitat on the Hill to look for the greatest number of different insects, birds, and mammals.

Spring

In spring when the water is high, look for leafy branches on the dam and whitish twigs along the pond edges. These signs will tell you the pond is currently occupied by Beaver. The bare twigs are cast-off after the bark is eaten. The delicate front feet of the Beaver are used for digging and for manipulating twigs as small as pencils. Its broad, webbed hind feet are used to propel it through the water. Its incisors are broad and orange and, as in most rodents, grow constantly; they are excellent chewing machines and signs of their activity are all around you. Predators of Beaver include coyotes, wolves, and otters.

Sit quietly by an active beaver flow at dusk and the curious residents will swim over to check you out, sometimes floating to within 20 feet. You may be able to watch a Beaver twirl twigs in its forepaws and munch the soft bark as if eating corn-on-the-cob. If you are *not* still enough you will see a demonstration of the way the Beaver uses its tail to produce a loud *'slap'* on the water as it quickly submerges and disappears, a distinctive Beaver warning sound.

A beaver flow is the best place to see two of the most striking ducks in North America, the *woody* and the *hoody*. The **Wood Duck** (*woody*) is one of the most beautiful ducks and a favorite of waterfowl hunters. The brilliant markings of the *drake* (male) are well known and the *hen* (female) has spectacular markings of silver teardrops on her wings and tail. Since its diet consists of vegetable matter such as acorns, beechnuts, and seeds of aquatic plants, people enjoy the Wood Duck as a tasty meal. Numbers of this species have increased in recent years as a result of season regulations and nesting box programs. The Wood Duck moves south for the winter months but returns early to select a nest site. The shrill call of the duck at dusk and dawn is a signal of the arrival of spring to the pond. Watch cavities in the dead trunks and you may be lucky enough to catch a glimpse of a young Wood Duck performing a death-defying 20-foot leap from the hole where it was hatched to the water surface below. The jump seems to be necessary to stimulate digestive activity in the ducklings.

The **Hooded Merganser** (*hoody*) is almost always seen in pairs on still waters in spring, diving for minnows. The drake is a striking black and white. He fans out his white crest like a hood in a mating display that gives him his name. The hen is brown and black. Beaver dams and resulting beaver ponds make ideal conditions for the hoody since the water is warm and productive for its prey; small fish.

Every beaver flow will be adopted by **Song Sparrows**. The male Sparrow proclaims a section of the flow as his by announcing it with song. The bird perches at the top of a small dead tree in the early spring morning and sings its loud, musical song starting with three strong notes, *'sweet-sweet-sweet'*.

Listen for the piercing, slurred *'kee-yurr'* call of the **Red-shouldered Hawk**. In early spring, this bird-of-prey returns from its winter range in the Southeastern U.S., establishes territory, constructs a large stick nest, and lays eggs. A Red-shouldered Hawk pair typically mates for life, and the same pair often reuses a nest for many years. The presence of this hawk confirms the richness, vitality, and remoteness of the area since it is quite sensitive to the activities of people. This hawk is listed by the New York State Department of Environmental Conservation as a Species of Special Concern.

If you are lucky you may see a large semi-aquatic shrew, the **Northern Water Shrew**, along both swift-flowing and quiet waters on the Hill. It takes patience to see this animal. Look for small footprints in fine silts and sands along stream edges. Wet prints on rocks will tell you that a shrew has been hunting in the area. A fringe of stiff hairs on its hind feet allows this shrew to run across the water surface, skating on the surface tension. The Northern Water Shrew dives to the bottom of a stream to look for food, and propelled by its slightly webbed hind toes, it is a very capable swimmer. This voracious shrew feeds on nymphs, larvae of stoneflies, mayflies, caddisflies, spiders, aquatic beetles, and even small fish.

If you are mole watching, you could see a mole that is unmistakable; the **Star-nosed Mole**. Its nose is decorated with a ring of 22 *nasal rays* (fleshy appendages) that perform a sensory function. The tail of both sexes of Star-nosed Moles swells annually in fall and spring, apparently with fat deposits to provide a temporary store of energy during the breeding season. This relatively large mole is also semi-aquatic, and can even be seen swimming and foraging under the ice during winter. Mounds, called *molehills*, are shallow tunnels used for foraging, and many are used only once. Molehills seem to be most evident when the air temperature is between 55 and 60 degrees F.

The mole responds to ground vibrations, so it is not easily observed unless you sit quietly near a small stream or marsh edge during the late fall, winter, or early spring. The mole has a unique way of burrowing, using its large, digging forefeet held perpendicular to its shoulders for a lateral-stroke. It can dig quickly and prefers soils where it can dig easily. The Star-nosed Mole can go straight up or down a vertical burrow. It is famous for being *'blind'*, but it can see, though its eyes are very small, because it spends all its time in dark burrow systems. Relatively little is known about this animal, although the mole is a major part of North American fauna.

Summer

After the spring runoff passes downstream, the pond levels start to drop, exposing a rich, organic muck layer around the edges that offends some noses with the odor of decaying vegetation. Look for Beaver and many other tracks in this mud ring to read a record of the activities of the previous night. You could see Beaver kits perfecting their swimming skills while the adults munch lush green shoots and ferns along the pond edge.

This is the time, when the waters are finally warm, to go wading in Tug Hill streams looking for salamanders, aquatic insects, crayfish, and mussels. In a good spot, with the right combination of flat rocks, clear water, and a protective tree canopy, you may find all four species of 'streamside salamanders'; the Mountain Dusky Salamander, the Northern Dusky Salamander, the Northern Two-Lined Salamander, and the Spring Salamander.

While all deposit their eggs in the water and spend the first part of their lives there as gill-breathing larvae, the adult Mountain Dusky Salamander may venture quite far from the stream bank. On rainy evenings you may even find it climbing in the foliage of ferns and shrubs searching for its invertebrate prey.

Its close relative, the Northern Dusky Salamander, rarely strays further than a few yards from the flowing brook, and typically is found right at the edge of the water.

The slender Two-lined Salamander, recognized by its bright yellow underside, tolerates a wider variety of ecological conditions. In moist woodlands following rains, Two-lined Salamanders may wander many yards from the creek edge.

The Spring Salamander attains the greatest size and bulk of the streamside salamanders, reaching lengths of over 8 inches. Try to catch these creatures (gently) from under rocks. Their speed and wriggling movements make it challenging. All these salamanders breathe entirely through their skin and must remain moist to survive.

Mussels and Clams belong to the group of animals known as Molluscs, a group that includes snails and slugs. Look for them in ponds and streams where they anchor themselves to the bottom in sand, mud, and clay. Freshwater Mussels and Clams are *bivalves* (they have a shell with two halves) and have a fleshy, burrowing foot. They use this foot to move their way through the bottom mud of ponds and streams. They circulate water through two tube-like siphons located at the rear or posterior end of the body, the narrower part of the shell. Water enters through the lower siphon. The water, carrying food and oxygen, passes over gills toward the mouth and then outward through the upper siphon.

You may get a thrill if you come upon a basking **Northern Water Snake**. You might almost step on this snake before you see it, its dark gray color blends into its surroundings so well. By the time you do see the snake, it is often poised to strike at your ankles. A large Northern Water Snake in a threatening posture within a foot of your leg can make your hair stand on end but, though it can bite, it is not poisonous, and is quite harmless. Just move away and let the snake have that space.

Listen for a common song coming from the shrubby tangles along the pond edge, *'witchity, witchity, witchity, witchity'*. The bird you hear is the **Common Yellowthroat**. Another colorful bird commonly found along creeks and ponds that announces its presence with a song is the **American Redstart**. Listen for a thin, *'tseet, tseet, tseet'*. Watch for its animated movements, as it droops its wings, fans its tail, and leaps into the air to catch insects.

By late May, insect repellent is required equipment for pond and creek watching. The body fluids of plants and animals make such a nutritious meal for organisms able to extract it, that it is no wonder there are so many insects that make their living this way. As any dweller on Tug Hill knows, the region is plagued by several types of biting flies that make it extremely difficult to enjoy the outdoors at certain times of the year. The most notorious of this cursed lot is the Black Fly, of which there are several species.

The Black Fly lays its eggs in sediments along the banks of creeks and streams in summer and fall. When the snow melts and fills the creeks the following spring, the eggs are washed into the water where their development begins. Fewer Black Flies are produced in a winter with lower than average snowfall because fewer eggs enter the water. The larva attaches to underwater rocks and feeds on organic material brought to it by the current. Following metamorphosis, the adult emerges from the stream, mates, and searches for a bloodmeal, usually from birds and mammals. Like the mosquito, only the female bites. The larvae provide an abundant food supply for stream fishes, and, believe it or not, most never survive to adulthood. People are probably among their favorite hosts, perhaps because there is little fur to deal with.

The most conspicuous insects at the pond edge are the dragonflies and damselflies. Try to keep up with them as they cut and dart around you. Look closely at a dragonfly, or *darning needle*; don't worry, it won't sting you or sew up your mouth. Like many insects, it is equipped with a fascinating array of adaptations to very specialized niches in the ecological community. The wings are made of an intricate lattice of struts, covered with a thin, clear skin built for strength and lightness. They are attached with multi-directional, mechanical-looking swivel joints for maneuverability. The legs are long and barbed for catching prey on the wing and holding it securely. The head, with its huge eyes, is balanced on a pinpoint neck.

Once you start looking at dragonflies you realize that there are dozens of different species, each with some refinement of basic dragonfly components adapted for individual purposes and each sporting brightly colored body parts. The giant **Green Darner** can have a 5 inch wingspan while some of the damselflies are the size of a pin. Much of the erratic activity of dragonflies is for the purpose of laying eggs. The eggs are deposited in many ways; dropped into water, attached to objects in water, deposited in gelatinous masses, or inserted in soft plant tissue underwater. After hatching, the nymphal stage may be as short as a month, or as long as 5 years. To emerge, the nymph crawls out of the water and attaches itself to a suitable surface. The adult emerges through a longitudinal split in the thorax or head. The immature insect is predaceous, feeding on protozoa, other insects, and in some rare cases, even fish. Prey is captured by means of the modified mouth and extensible *labium* (lip). This labium grasps the prey and then retracts, bringing the prey to the *mandibles* (jaws).

Dragonflies are distinct from damselflies in a variety of ways. Dragonflies are strong fliers. The hindwings of dragonfly adults are broader at the base and held horizontally or slightly depressed at rest. Their heads are almost all eyes, but the eyes do not project from the sides of the head. Damselflies have wings of equal size, narrow at the base and held vertically at rest. Their eyes are bulbous and stick out from the sides of the head. Damselflies are weaker fliers. The immature forms differ in that the dragonfly nymphs are robust and the damselfly nymphs are slender, with paddle-like gills.

Fall

Return to the flow in fall to see frenzied Beaver activity as the animals are preparing for winter. You can quite easily watch a Beaver augment the dam, work on the lodge, and put down the winter food cache.

Look for a large area of twigs poking out of the water near the lodge; evidence that the lodge will be occupied through the coming winter. The sticks are anchored in the mud at the pond bottom where the Beaver can get at them beneath the ice. Two-year-old young are chased away by the female and must disperse to find their own territory. If you find a new site being developed by one of these outcasts, you are in for a show as the newcomer works feverishly to beat the coming cold weather.

Winter

Walk out onto the pond when the ice allows and find the beaver lodge. A Beaver spends the winter in the lodge, safe under ice and snow, feeding on its underwater cache. It swims out of the lodge through an underwater tunnel, chews off a branch, tows it into the lodge, and eats it on a shelf it has built just above the water surface between the tunnel and the higher den. Look at the top of the lodge, if it is active there will be a vent hole where the snow has been melted by body heat. Look for frost crystals on the sticks around the vent for evidence of the passage of warm air from breathing and body heat. Put your ear over the opening and listen for squeaking and munching sounds from within. You may hear the activities of the *kits* (Beaver young) that are born in January.

Walk along the frozen rivers and look for the tracks of other aquatic mammals. If your timing is right you could see the tracks and slides of a **River Otter**. Other otter *signs* (evidence of the animal's activities) include *toilet* sites, *spraints* (scent-markings) near landing areas on prominent rocks or logs extending into the water, and *haul-outs* where a wet otter lands and rolls to groom and dry out its fur. Otters are abundant along remote streams and lakes, but they are shy and rarely seen. Look for an otter from dawn to midmorning and during evening hours. Trout fishermen often think the otter is competing with them for Trout. However, studies have shown that the otter prefers slow-moving fish like suckers, dace, shiners, and sculpins. Other important foods are frogs and other amphibians, aquatic insects, and crayfish. The otter is very intelligent and strong and can move underwater rocks and boulders to search for prey. The graceful movement of an otter as it swims with its head above water or dives for fish, or fun, is a beautiful sight. Habitat destruction, acid rain damage, and pollution of aquatic habitat all jeopardize the otter population.

A relative of the otter, the **Mink** is fairly easy to see in winter. The Mink is a medium-sized member of the weasel family with a famously luxuriant, dark-brown coat and a white chin. Look for tracks indicating Mink activity and watch the area. Winter nests of Muskrat fur indicate that a Mink will eat Muskrat where this marsh-loving rodent is common.

These furbearing mammals attract trappers to flows and creeks to harvest their pelts. Trapping with proper management techniques poses no threat to the populations. Harvesting a sustainable yield of pelts can keep populations healthy and provide an important supplement to the local economy.

ILLUSTRATIONS

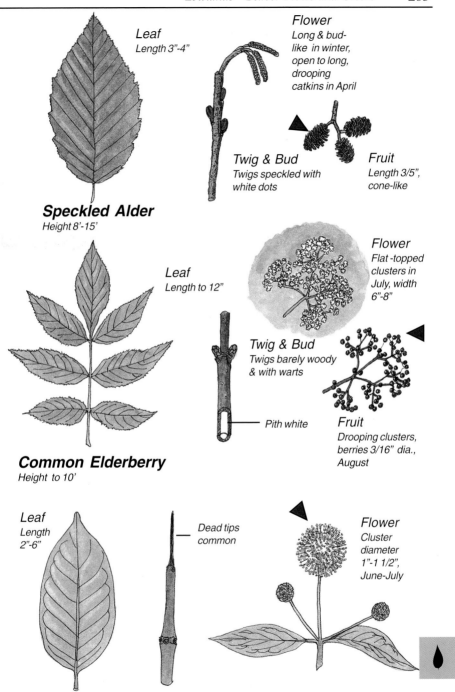

Leaf
Length 3"-4"

Flower
Long & bud-like in winter, open to long, drooping catkins in April

Twig & Bud
Twigs speckled with white dots

Fruit
Length 3/5", cone-like

Speckled Alder
Height 8'-15'

Leaf
Length to 12"

Flower
Flat-topped clusters in July, width 6"-8"

Twig & Bud
Twigs barely woody & with warts

Pith white

Fruit
Drooping clusters, berries 3/16" dia., August

Common Elderberry
Height to 10'

Leaf
Length 2"-6"

Dead tips common

Flower
Cluster diameter 1"-1 1/2", June-July

Buttonbush
Height to 8'

Twig & Bud
Buds inconspicuous

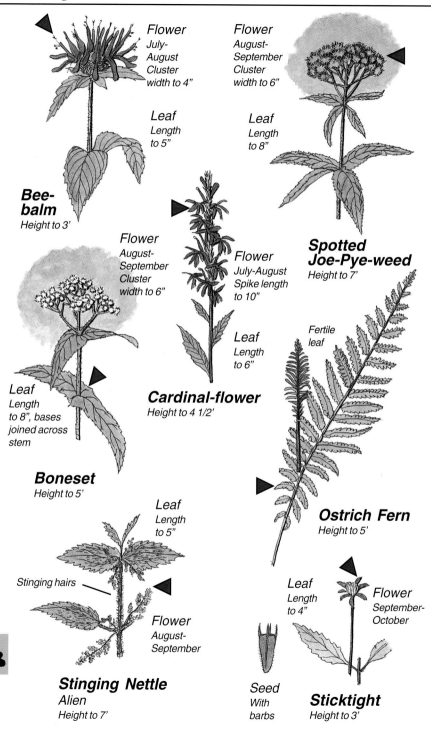

Flower
July-
August
Cluster
width to 4"

Leaf
Length
to 5"

**Bee-
balm**
Height to 3'

Flower
August-
September
Cluster
width to 6"

Leaf
Length
to 8"

**Spotted
Joe-Pye-weed**
Height to 7'

Flower
August-
September
Cluster
width to 6"

Leaf
Length
to 8", bases
joined across
stem

Boneset
Height to 5'

Flower
July-August
Spike length
to 10"

Leaf
Length
to 6"

Cardinal-flower
Height to 4 1/2'

Fertile
leaf

Ostrich Fern
Height to 5'

Leaf
Length
to 5"

Stinging hairs

Flower
August-
September

Stinging Nettle
Alien
Height to 7'

Leaf
Length
to 4"

Flower
September-
October

Seed
With
barbs

Sticktight
Height to 3'

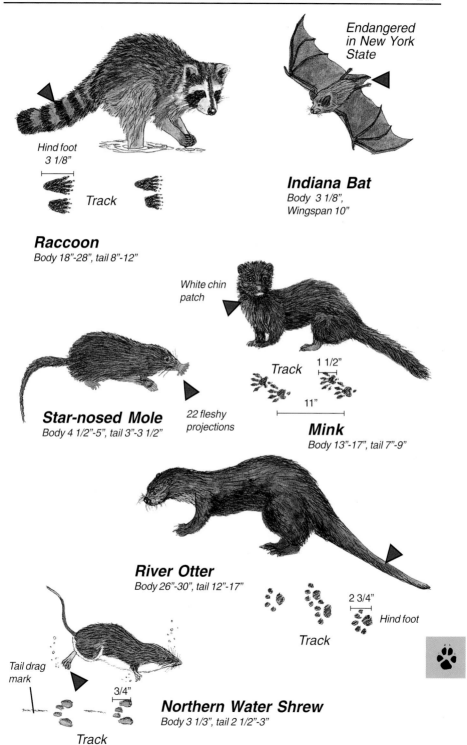

Indiana Bat
Endangered in New York State
Body 3 1/8",
Wingspan 10"

Raccoon
Body 18"-28", tail 8"-12"
Hind foot 3 1/8"
Track

Star-nosed Mole
Body 4 1/2"-5", tail 3"-3 1/2"
22 fleshy projections

Mink
White chin patch
Body 13"-17", tail 7"-9"
Track
1 1/2"
11"

River Otter
Body 26"-30", tail 12"-17"
Track
2 3/4"
Hind foot

Northern Water Shrew
Body 3 1/3", tail 2 1/2"-3"
Tail drag mark
3/4"
Track

Osprey
Length 22"-25", Wingspan 58"-72"
Hovers over large water bodies,
dives & plunges on fish, feet first

Wings
angled in
flight

Belted Kingfisher
Length 13"
Plunges straight into water after
small fish

Colored
bands on
breast

Hen

Drake

Hen

Drake

Wood Duck
Length 18 1/2"
Pair & mate on small ponds &
streams in April

Hooded Merganser
Length 18"
Mate at same time & place as Wood Duck

Crest ▶

Cedar Waxwing
Length 7 1/4"
Feeds in small flocks

Red-shouldered Hawk
Length 19", Wingspan 40"
Perches along small streams & flows, calls as it soars a series of sharp, single notes

◀ Banded tail

Song Sparrow
Length 6 1/4"
Sings from same perch day after day

Common Yellowthroat
Length 5"
Flits along low stems of cattails & shrubs

Black mask

Colored patches

American Redstart
Length 5 1/4"
Active in shrubs & trees along water, fans its tail and wings when perched

Common Loon
Length 32"
Dives to feed & when nervous, swims great distances under water

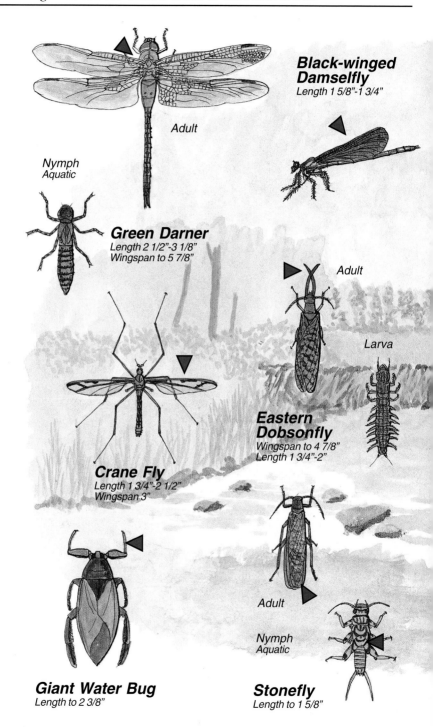

**Black-winged
Damselfly**
Length 1 5/8"-1 3/4"

Adult

*Nymph
Aquatic*

Green Darner
Length 2 1/2"-3 1/8"
Wingspan to 5 7/8"

Adult

Larva

**Eastern
Dobsonfly**
Wingspan to 4 7/8"
Length 1 3/4"-2"

Crane Fly
Length 1 3/4"-2 1/2"
Wingspan 3"

Adult

*Nymph
Aquatic*

Giant Water Bug
Length to 2 3/8"

Stonefly
Length to 1 5/8"

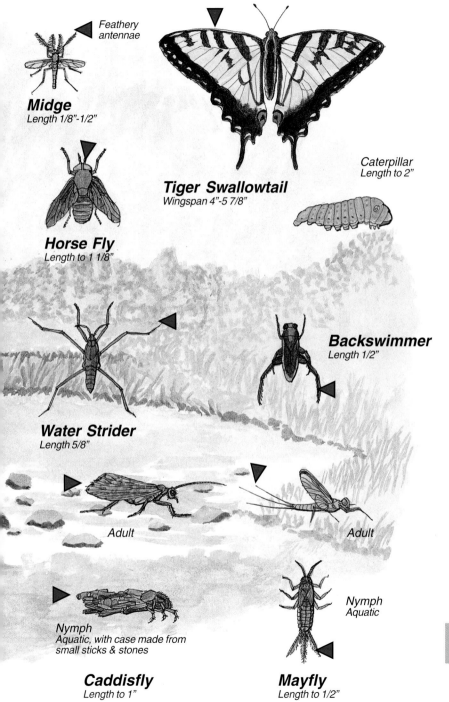

Midge
Length 1/8"-1/2"

Feathery antennae

Tiger Swallowtail
Wingspan 4"-5 7/8"

Caterpillar
Length to 2"

Horse Fly
Length to 1 1/8"

Backswimmer
Length 1/2"

Water Strider
Length 5/8"

Adult

Adult

Nymph
Aquatic

Nymph
Aquatic, with case made from
small sticks & stones

Caddisfly
Length to 1"

Mayfly
Length to 1/2"

Northern Water Snake
Length 22"-53"

Northern Two-lined Salamander *Length 2 1/2"-4 3/4"*

Yellow belly

Markings highly variable

Northern Dusky Salamander
Length 2 1/2"-5 1/2"

Spring Salamander
Length 4 1/4"-8 5/8"

Aquatic phase, length 2 5/8"-5 1/2"

Red Eft phase (land form),
length 1 3/8"-3 3/8"

Common Snapping Turtle
*Length 8"-12" common,
to 18 1/2"*

Red-spotted Newt

FACTS, TIPS, AND LORE

FACTS, TIPS, AND LORE
BEAVER FLOWS AND CREEKS

SHRUBS

Pussy Willow   (not illustrated)

The Pussy Willow is the shrub that is a harbinger of spring. Every child is familiar with the fuzzy buds of this large shrub or small tree as they begin to open. The early, fuzzy buds are the flower buds.

Common Elderberry

This shrub has flat-topped clusters of fruit that are a well-known sight in late August. Common Elderberry fruit is used in jam, jelly, wine, and pies. More than 40 species of birds are known to eat the berries.

Arrowwood   (not illustrated)

Arrowwood is named for the straight suckering shoots that were used for arrow shafts by Native Americans. This shrub is easily recognized in summer by the flat-topped clusters of creamy white flowers. The fruit is eaten by many species of wildlife.

Speckled Alder

Speckled Alder is named for the white *lenticels* (speckles) on the twigs. These speckles make identification easy in any season. Moose, deer, Muskrat, and rabbit browse the twigs. This plant improves the soil by releasing nitrogen in a form that can be used by other plants.

HERBACEOUS PLANTS

Boneset

The name of this plant comes from its use as a cure by Native Americans and others for *'break-bone fever'*. The abundance of Boneset varies with the cycle of the beaver flow. At times when the meadow is rejuvenating, Boneset may cover a wide zone between open water and the shore.

Bluejoint Grass   (not illustrated)

Bluejoint Grass is often found in large populations in wet meadows and open swamps, especially in old beaver flows. The plant was named for the bluish joints or nodes along the stem. Bluejoint Grass grows from 1 ½ - 4 ½ feet tall.

Spotted Joe-Pye-weed

The pink flower clusters of Spotted Joe-Pye-weed are a good place to look for beetles and other insects. This plant grows in old beaver flows together with Boneset, goldenrods, and other flowering plants to make a showy display in the interim period of the cycle of Beaver activity.

Stinging Nettle

One of the hazards of wading through thick streamside vegetation is getting *'stings'* on your arms and face from Stinging Nettle. Being flogged with nettle was a strange practice once used as a cure for rheumatism. The nettle plant produces fibers like flax that can be made into cloth and cordage.

Sticktight (Beggar-ticks)

Another streamside plant that will assail you is the Sticktight. The hitchhikers all over your pants and shoelaces are seeds, and you are part of the dispersal strategy of this plant.

Cardinal-flower

The blazing scarlet color of Cardinal-flower stands out in the crowd of weedy plants. Watch for hummingbirds visiting the flowers.

MOSSES AND FERNS

Brook Moss   (not illustrated)

Brook Moss grows attached to rocks in swiftly moving water. The plants are long and trailing, and when many are on a rock, it can look somewhat like a person's hair trailing in the water. This moss has a rather fishy smell when it dries.

Ostrich Fern

This large fern was named for the long, graceful leaves that are shaped like an Ostrich feather.

MAMMALS

Indiana Bat   *Endangered in New York State*

Found only in the Eastern United States, this small bat migrates in winter to one of only *seven* caves! This bat is very sensitive to disturbance while hibernating. In a single incident when a winter flood inundated their hibernation cave, 60 percent of the known population was killed. In summer, the Indiana Bat roosts and raises its young in a hollow limb or under loose bark. At dusk, look near the foliage of trees along small streams for this bat as it feeds on flies and moths. The tunnel-like opening along a stream is a key habitat feature for this bat because it still provides enough insects to enable pregnancy and lactation even in cool years when insect populations are low. People can help protect the Indiana Bat by maintaining the streamside forests that provide summer habitat.

Raccoon

The Raccoon makes its home in a hollow tree, a fissure in rocks, or in the habitations of people (chimneys, attics, and any other place that is like a tree hollow). The Raccoon is usually inactive (sleeping in its den) from December through March. It may forage late in the winter, even in deep snow, if the temperature is above freezing for several days. Follow the tracks and you can find the den. After emerging from its winter sleep, a female will mate and choose a different den for raising her family. Listen for a unique, high-pitched *'chitter'* that will tell you there may be a Raccoon den nearby. The density of the Raccoon population can be over 20 animals per square mile. A Raccoon feels along a streambed with its hands underwater, searching for crayfish, frogs, or fish. This activity is the cause of the myth that the Raccoon washes its food. A Raccoon will eat almost anything, including all fruits and nuts, corn and other grains, weeds and fungus, aquatic animals, small mammals, and birds. Large individuals weigh up to 30 pounds.

Mink

The Mink is never far from a small stream or other water body. It is a very active animal, normally nocturnal, but it can be observed hunting for frogs, fish, aquatic insects, and other animals at any time of the day or night. The female Mink makes her nest under a tangle of tree roots along the bank, in a muskrat lodge, or in a natural den cavity. Here, she gives birth to 3-6 young around April. In the fall, the young disperse to new home ranges.

River Otter

The River Otter is an aquatic, playful member of the weasel family. It gives birth in the spring to 2 to 4 young in a burrow near the water.

BIRDS

Common Loon

Listening to a Common Loon calling at night is a rare wilderness treat. Since nesting sites are very susceptible to disturbance by the activities of people, such as boating, this bird requires a large uninhabited water body to nest. It also needs a large body of water to take flight. Common Loons can often be seen during migration, resting and feeding on the Salmon River Reservoir. The bird is recognized in flight by its trailing feet and rapid wing beat. This aquatic bird will sometimes land on a wet highway, mistaking it for a river. It can not regain flight from a solid surface since its legs are too far back on its body to support it in an upright position.

Wood Duck

This duck breeds on Tug Hill and nests in holes in trees or nest boxes put out by people specifically for Wood Ducks. The ducklings feed extensively on insects of all kinds early in their life.

Hooded Merganser

This duck is the smallest of the fish-eating ducks. All these ducks have serrate bills for capturing and holding fish. The Hooded Merganser breeds on the Hill, and like the Wood Duck, it nests in tree cavities and nest boxes. In places it no doubt competes with the *'woody'* for nest boxes and will lay eggs on top of Wood Duck eggs. This duck is a very fast flier that fishes for minnows in the many small open wetlands, small creeks, and river systems on the Hill. The Hooded Merganser is hunted, though as is the case with all fish ducks and other diving ducks, its edibility is debatable.

Osprey (Fish Hawk)

The Osprey breeds on Tug Hill near the Salmon River Reservoir and probably near Whetstone Gulf State Park. The bird can be seen near large rivers and lakes where it feeds exclusively on fish. The population has increased in recent years since the use of DDT and PCBs has been banned. The Osprey is often incorrectly identified as a Bald Eagle. The Osprey flies with a kink or crook in its wings, while the Bald Eagle flies with flat wings, and Eagles have a solid white tail.

Belted Kingfisher

Look for the Belted Kingfisher sitting on a tree limb above a stream, where it watches the water surface for signs of minnow activity. It dives into the water beak first and captures a minnow, lands on a perch, and stuns the wiggling fish by slamming it against a branch before swallowing it whole. The Belted Kingfisher nest is built in a tunnel burrowed as deep as 10 feet into a bank along a stream. The bird can be seen or heard during winter as long as open water and fish are available.

REPTILES

Common Snapping Turtle

The closest thing to a giant reptile on Tug Hill is the Common Snapping Turtle. It seems that everybody has a story about a huge snapper that bit their oar in two or dragged an entire family of ducks into the murky depths. While these stories are often exaggerations, there is no question that the snapper is a powerful beast, and when it reaches adult size, it reigns supreme in the lake, pond, or stream. An adult snapper's shell can be 18 inches long and the turtle can weigh 35 pounds or more. Watch for the Common Snapping Turtle in June when the female leaves the safety of the pond to bury her eggs in gravel flats or the shoulders of roads.

Northern Water Snake

The behavior of this snake is aggressive when cornered; it will flatten its body, lunge, bite, and spray a foul musk, but it is not poisonous. There are no poisonous water snakes north of southern Virginia and there are no naturally occurring poisonous snakes of any kind on Tug Hill. This snake preys on fish and frogs.

INSECTS

Black-winged Damselfly

Watch for this damselfly in summer as it flits from place to place on streamside vegetation along a slow moving stream. It flies much like a butterfly and often mills about with a group of other damselflies. The Black-winged Damselfly *naiad* (aquatic young form) is pale brown with dark brown markings and yellow-brown or orange legs. Adults eat small insects including aphids, the naiads feed on small aquatic insects. Females force small eggs, singly, into soft, underwater plant stem tissue.

FISHES

Brook Trout   (not illustrated)

On Tug Hill, Brook Trout can be found in the cold, clear headwaters of most streams. The Brook Trout, the state fish of New York , thrives in water having a low temperature and high oxygen content. Unlike Brown and Rainbow Trout, the Brook Trout is native to Tug Hill. A short life span (about 5 years maximum) and a cold water environment combine to limit the size of the Brook Trout to about 12 inches in Tug Hill populations. The fish matures at about 2 years of age and spawns in the fall. The female constructs a nest on the gravelly bottom of a stream. Young trout feed primarily on immature insects. Old fish eat a variety of insects, worms, crustaceans, and small fish. The practice of leaving undisturbed areas along streams in logged woodlots helps to keep the water cold and prevents the siltation that reduces food supply and destroys spawning areas for Brook Trout.

Cutlips Minnow   (not illustrated)

This fish, named for its three-lobed lower jaw, is a slow moving, bottom dweller preferring pools in fast-flowing streams. The Cutlips Minnow eats the eyes of other minnows. The male builds a nest by transporting stones in his mouth. Watch a gravelly stream bottom in May or June to witness nest-building activities.

Whetstone Gulf

GULFS AND BOGS

VERIFYING CHARACTERISTICS

- **Bog** – No flowing water. A wetland where the water and nutrients enter only as a result of rainfall. Plants grow faster than they can decompose, resulting in accumulation of peat. Floating mat of sedges and mosses. Methane smell when disturbed.
- **Gulf** - Deep, steep-sided gorges, the major gulfs are located on east and north sides of Hill. Exposed sedimentary rock in horizontal layers.

"Tug Hill Country embraces not only the plateau itself, but all the vast regions that are watered by and drained by the tumultuous streams that come down from its flinty slopes, and through its rocky gorges."

from "Tug Hill Country" by Harold E. Samson

BOGS

Bog is the name given to many wet areas where Sphagnum Moss is present on the Hill, but most of these areas are more correctly called fens. The difference is that fens are usually located along the edges of streams, wetlands, or ponds with flowing water. There is no water flowing into or out of bogs. True bogs are relatively rare on the Hill. Both bogs and fens host unique plants and animals, many of which are also rare. It is best not to walk on a bog since the vegetation is fragile and you could fall through. If you do explore one, however, do it carefully and infrequently, and do not collect the rare plants and animals. Most of the inhabitants of bogs are protected by law.

Look for the carnivorous plants; the Sundew, Pitcher Plant, and Bladderwort. These plants trap and digest insects for the nutrients that are in scant supply in a bog environment. They can also be found in fens. You will get wet knees looking for **Sundew**, since the plants are tiny. Hairs that ring the round leaves are tipped with droplets of a liquid that looks like dew. Unwary insects discover too late that the liquid is sticky and they are trapped. The hairs fold inward to encase the insect, and the leaf secretes enzymes to dissolve the insect into plant nourishing nutrients. The **Pitcher Plant** holds a reservoir of water that attracts insects. When they turn around to walk out, they find that they are trying to walk up against a barricade of downward pointing hairs. They eventually fall into the water and are digested. To find one, look for the odd, reddish flower of the plant standing above the surrounding grasses and sedges on a long, stiff stalk. The **Bladderwort** is a small plant living in puddles in the bog. The underwater leaf stalks have small bristle-tipped bladders that open when triggered by a small arthropod and suck in water, arthropod and all. The trap door closes and the prey is digested.

Sphagnum Moss is the primary component of the floating mat that supports these unusual plants and forms peat after centuries of accumulation. Sphagnum stems may be over a foot long, but only the upper portion is green and growing. Poke below this and you will see that the stem gradually loses color, becoming white and then brown; below that you will see that the stem has begun to decompose. Sphagnum can control the succession of the ecological community by creating acidic conditions in which only certain species can grow. The acidic conditions also slow the decomposition rate, which causes peat formation and preserves animals and people that fell into bogs thousands of years ago. If you look closely at sphagnum 'gardens' you will see differences in color and texture between plant masses. There are 18 different species of sphagnum native to Tug Hill, but you have to be a very dedicated sphagnum student to name them.

Late in the fall look for **Cranberries** while you are kneeling in the sphagnum. The many fascinating discoveries that await you in the bog make it well worth while to get a little wet.

GULFS

Seventeen major gulfs drain water and cold air from the Hill. They show on satellite photos as shadowy gashes that snake back and forth as they cut through the edge of the escarpments. Several of the gulfs feature waterfalls and cascades tumbling over the harder strata of the sedimentary rock layers. The walls of the gulfs display part of the geological record of the formation of the Hill. The most spectacular falls are Deer Creek Falls and Salmon River Falls.

Whetstone Gulf is probably the best known gulf since it is a State Park. Whetstone Gulf is about 2 miles long and 300 feet deep.

Bear Gulf, Shingle Gulf, and Inman Gulf are located on the western fringe of the Hill and drain into Sandy Creek. Inman Gulf is at least 6 miles long and 200-300 feet deep. Lorraine Gulf, Totman Gulf, and Mooney Gulf also drain westward into South Sandy Creek. Lorraine Gulf is more than 200 feet deep in places. Gulfs on the northern part of the eastern escarpment: Roaring Brook, Whetstone Gulf, House Creek, Mill Creek, and Olmstead Brook drain into the Black River. Gulfs of the southern part of the eastern escarpment: Lansing Kill, Chase Creek, Clark Brook, and Stringer Brook, drain into the Mohawk River.

The formation of gulfs began when torrents of water melting from the last glacial stage washed over the east and north edges of the Hill and carved deep notches through the sandstone and into the underlying siltstones and soft shales. Streams fed by abundant rainfall and snowmelt continued cutting back into the Hill over the centuries, cutting downward through the soft rock and carrying it away as sediment. The sides of the gorges are so steep because the amount of rock removed by downward cutting in the soft shales is greater than the amount falling off the harder sandstone sidewalls over the same time period. Gulfs can be dangerous since the edges are steep, the vertical drop in many cases is more than 100 feet, and the rock is soft and very unstable. Stay well away from the top edge, because it could be undercut, and do not climb the sidewalls. Many of the gulfs are on private lands. Please respect the property rights of the owners by asking permission before entering their property.

The draining effect of cold air that reduces killing frosts and the shelter provided by the gulfs allows plants more common in southerly communities to thrive. Red Oak trees grow in the gulfs but do not thrive above the rim, they can be found as far up Inman Gulf as Barnes Corners. The variable rock layers, from fine shale to limestone, provide a variety of soil and moisture regimes that favor plants that are uncommon elsewhere on the Hill. Watch here for an unusual bird for Tug Hill, the **Louisiana Waterthrush**. This bird is a regular inhabitant of the gulfs but is uncommon on the Hill. You can also scan the snags and cliffs along the rim for hawk or raven nests.

The gulfs present a dramatic expression of the height of the elevated lands that form the Hill.

Pitcher Plant

ILLUSTRATIONS

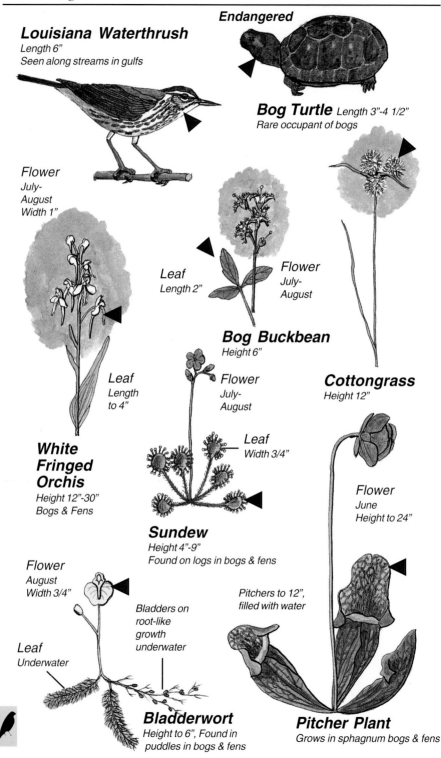

Endangered

Louisiana Waterthrush
Length 6"
Seen along streams in gulfs

Bog Turtle Length 3"-4 1/2"
Rare occupant of bogs

Flower
July-
August
Width 1"

Leaf
Length 2"

Flower
July-
August

Bog Buckbean
Height 6"

Leaf
Length
to 4"

Flower
July-
August

Cottongrass
Height 12"

Leaf
Width 3/4"

White
Fringed
Orchis
Height 12"-30"
Bogs & Fens

Sundew
Height 4"-9"
Found on logs in bogs & fens

Flower
June
Height to 24"

Flower
August
Width 3/4"

Bladders on
root-like
growth
underwater

Pitchers to 12",
filled with water

Leaf
Underwater

Bladderwort
Height to 6", Found in
puddles in bogs & fens

Pitcher Plant
Grows in sphagnum bogs & fens

FACTS, TIPS, AND LORE

FACTS, TIPS, AND LORE
GULFS AND BOGS

HERBACEOUS PLANTS

Sundew

Called a *'bloodthirsty little miscreant'* by the early botanist Neltje Blanchan in 1901, Sundew is a carnivorous plant that digests insects in order to get the nitrogen that is in short supply in the bog environment. The plant is named for drops of sticky resin that tip the ring of hairs around the leaf and look like dewdrops. You can feed an insect to a Sundew leaf and watch the feeding process, if you have the patience.

Bog Buckbean

Bog Buckbean grows on the sphagnum mat in bogs. The leaves of this plant are food for the larvae of the rare Bog Buckmoth. If you see a large black and white moth with an orange patch on its abdomen, notify the Endangered Species Unit of the NYSDEC, and do not disturb the insect. Only two populations of the moths are known to exist near the Hill but scientists are on the lookout for other populations.

Pitcher Plant

This is a unique plant that is well known for its pitcher-shaped leaves that hold little reservoirs of water. The pools of water are miniature ecosystems, hosting activities of many interrelated creatures. Look at a drop under a microscope and you may see a sampling of the residents.

Bladderwort

Bladderwort is found in puddles on the surface of the floating mat in bogs. The leaves of the plant float below the water surface and the bladders are attached to the underwater stems. The flowers are borne on a 4 inch stem that rises above the water level.

MOSSES

Sphagnum Moss (Peat Moss) (not illustrated)

This moss was the main attraction of bogs in the past because of its many uses. Sphagnum Moss is a moss with a unique appearance; it has a bunch of young branches at the tip of its stems that form a tufted head, and it has bundles of branches along the sides of the stem. Sphagnum Moss is legendary for its water holding capacity; some species can hold up to 20 times their dry weight in water. The moss is used in the nursery and craft trades, and as fuel in the form of cut peat. Native Americans used sphagnum for *'diapers'*, and boot liners. Sphagnum was used in WWI as a surgical dressing because of its ability to decrease bacterial infections and heal wounds. Wound healing was better with sphagnum than with sterile white bandages. This super-absorbent moss can also be used to treat moderate oil spills, for small-scale sewage treatment, and to remove acid dyes and toxic metals from industrial effluent.

REPTILES

Bog Turtle   *Endangered in New York State*

The Bog Turtle is the smallest turtle in New York. It is unclear whether any significant populations occur within the Tug Hill region, however a single individual was captured in a western Oswego County pond a few years ago. If you find a Bog Turtle please do not disturb it and report the sighting to the Endangered Species Unit of NYSDEC.

PART FOUR
APPENDIX

GLOSSARY

adaptation - the process by which species become better suited to their location.

adventitious rooting - growing roots at points where branches touch the ground.

alien - species that is not native to an area.

biennial plant - a plant that matures over two seasons.

canopy – 'ceiling' over the forest formed by the intermeshed uppermost branches.

carnivorous – feeding on animals.

carrion - dead animals.

catkins - caterpillar-shaped clusters of tiny flowers or fruits.

chrysalis - cocoon-like structure that houses a developing butterfly.

climax forest – an association of trees that has reached equilibrium with environmental conditions, the final stage of plant succession.

colonial nester – a species that nests in close proximity to many other mating pairs of its kind.

crown – the top leafy perimeter of an individual tree.

dieback - a general decline caused by air pollution, insect pests, or other causes.

diversity – the existence of different species of plants and animals.

drumlins - hills shaped like upside-down spoons that were formed by glaciers.

emetic – causing vomiting.

ephemeral – lasting for a short time.

erratic – stone or boulder brought to an area by a glacier.

exotic – a species that is not native to an area.

extirpated – eliminated from a natural range or area.

fern-allies - plants that are closely related to ferns.

forest duff - the decaying organic layer next to the soil on the floor of a forest.

fragmentation - subdivision of large forests into smaller pieces by road building and clearing.

gall - a growth on a plant resulting from a fungus or egg-laying or feeding of mites and insect larvae.

glacial till - unsorted rock and soil deposited by a glacier.

haul-out – place where a wet otter lands and rolls to groom and dry out its fur.

heartwood - the non-growing wood that makes up most of a tree trunk.

herbaceous plant - a non-woody plant.

herbivorous – feeding on plants.

inflorescence - flower cluster.

isopod – member of the order *Isopoda*, a group terrestrial and aquatic crustaceans.

labium – lip or lip-like part.

lenticel – corky bump on a plant stem that functions to exchange gases.

luciferin – the protein responsible for producing light in fireflies.

mandible - upper or lower part of a birds bill or mouthpart of an insect.

mantling – covering a catch with hunched wings.

marsupial – a female animal that has a pouch for carrying its undeveloped young.

mesic forest - forest that is growing on moist, well-drained soils.

metamorphosis – change from one form or shape to another.

mobbing - excited gathering of several birds to drive away or confuse a bird of prey.

monoculture – planting of one species over a contiguous area.

morph - variation in a bird's plumage color unrelated to sex or season.

mucilaginous – soft and slimy.

naiad - aquatic nymphal stage of certain insects.

neotropical migrant – bird species that migrates from North America to Central or South America.

nest predation - intrusion on or laying eggs in the nest of one species of bird by another.

niche - specific portion of the cover or food supply available in a habitat.

nit - the egg, or young of a louse.

node - swollen place on a stem, especially at the leaf joints.

nymph – the young of an insect undergoing metamorphosis.

parasite – an organism that lives on or in another organism and takes nutrients from it.

pellet - regurgitated inedible portions of bird meals in the form of hairy, papery clumps.

perennial - a non-woody plant that lives from year to year by growing new shoots from its roots.

petiole - the stalk of a leaf.

photosynthesis - the process that green plants use to convert sunlight to energy.

pioneer species - plant that invades open areas after a disturbance like fire or logging.

plant succession - the progression of plant communities from field to forest.

precocial – having survival skills at an early age.

pupate – enter the dormant stage of development in a cocoon.

rhizome - underground stem that sends out roots and shoots.
saprophyte - a plant that obtains nutrients from decaying plant
    material.
sapwood - the growing layer of wood just beneath the bark.
scat - animal droppings.
sucker - tree shoot that sprouts from the underground parts of older
    trees.
vernal pool - temporary pools in low areas of the forest.
vertebrate - having a backbone.

BIBLIOGRAPHY

Borror, Donald J., and Richard E. White, 1970. *A Field Guide to Insects, America, North of Mexico.* The Peterson Field Guide Series. New York: Houghton Mifflin Co.

Chapman, William K., Valerie A. Chapman, Alan E. Bessette, Arleen Rainis Bessette, Douglas R. Pens, 1998. *Wildflowers of New York.* Syracuse, N.Y.: Syracuse University Press.

Cobb, Boughton, 1963. *A Field Guide to the Ferns.* The Peterson Field Guide Series. Boston, Ma.: Houghton Mifflin Co.

Conant, Roger, 1991 (3rd ed.). *A Field Guide to Reptiles and Amphibians, Eastern and Central North America.* Boston, Ma. : Houghton Mifflin Co.

Graves, Arthur Harmount, 1984 (revised ed.). *Illustrated Guide to Trees and Shrubs.* New York: Dover Publications, Inc.

Harrison, Hal H., 1975. *A Field Guide to the Bird's Nests, United States East of the Mississippi River.* The Peterson Field Guide Series. Boston, Ma.: Houghton Mifflin Co.

Kricher, John C., and Gordon Morrison, 1988. *A Field Guide to Eastern Forests.* The Peterson Field Guide Series. Boston, Ma.: Houghton Mifflin Co.

Murie, Olaus J., 1974 (2nd ed.). *A Field Guide to Animal Tracks.* The Peterson Field Guide Series. Boston, Ma.: Houghton Mifflin Co.

Opler, Paul A., and Vichai Malikul, 1992. *A Field Guide to Eastern Butterflies.* The Peterson Field Guide Series. New York: Houghton Mifflin Co.

Petrides, George A., 1972 (2nd ed.). *A Field Guide to Trees and Shrubs.* The Peterson Field Guide Series. Boston, Ma.: Houghton Mifflin Co.

Reschke, Carol, 1990. *Ecological Communities of New York State.* New York State Department of Environmental Conservation.

Stokes, Donald and Lillian, 1996. *Stokes Field Guide to Birds, Eastern Region*. Toronto: Little, Brown and Co.

Werner, Robert G., 1980. *Freshwater Fishes of New York State*. Syracuse, N.Y.: Syracuse University Press.

Whitaker, John O., 1996 (2nd ed.). *National Audubon Society Field Guide to North American Mammals.* New York : Knopf.

Tug Hill Working Lands 1991. The Tug Hill Commission and Tug Hill Tomorrow, Inc.

Neelands, R.W., 1968. *Important Trees of Eastern Forests.* U.S. Department of Agriculture - Forest Service.

INDEX

Entries in normal type are found in the *Narratives*, bold type entries
are *Illustrations*, and entries in italics are found in *Facts, Tips, and Lore.*

Alder, Speckled **205,** *215*
American Painted Lady **107,** *114*
American Pelecinid **64**
Anemone, Canada **178,** *114*
Ant, Allegheny Mound **87,** *95*
Antlion 53, **64**
Arrowwood *215*
Arum, Arrow **161**
Ash, White **29,** *40*
Aspen
       Bigtooth **84,** *91*
       Quaking 81, **84,** *91*
Backswimmer **211**
Banded Purple 36
Basswood, American **59**
Bat
       Indiana **207,** *217*
       Little Brown *137*
Bazzania, Three-lobed *166*
Beaver **194,** *195*
Bee-balm **206**
Bee, Carpenter *139*
Beech
       American **28,** *39*
       Blue **85,** *92*
Beetle
       Carrion *141*
       Ground **106, 126**
       June *141*
       Ladybug **106,** *114*
       Leaf **106**
       Predacious Diving **181**
       Red Milkweed **106**
       Six-spotted Green
              Tiger 81, **87**
       Whirligig **181,** *193*
Birch
       Gray 79, **84,** *91*
       Yellow **28,** *40*

Bittern, American **179,** *189*
Black Currant, American *41*
Black Huckleberry *185*
Blackberry *92*
Blackbird, Red-winged 172, **179,**
     190
Bladderwort 224, **228,** *231*
Bloodroot **31,** *42*
Blue Cohosh **31**
Blue Flag **178,** *187*
Blueberry, Highbush *111*
Bluebird, Eastern 118, **129**
Bobcat *73*
Bobolink 119, **129**
Boneset **206,** *215*
Buckbean, Bog **228,** *231*
Buckeye **106**
Bug
       Giant Water **210**
       Sow *48*
Bullfrog 172, **180,** *191*
Bull-thistle **126,** *133*
Bumblebee *139*
Bunchberry **61**
Bunting, Indigo **105**
Burdock, Common **125,** *133*
Butterfly-weed **104,** *111*
Buttonbush **205**
Caddisfly **211**
Canada Mayflower **60**
Cardinal-flower **206,** *216*
Carolina Spring Beauty **31,** *42*
Catbird, Gray **105**
Caterpillar
       Eastern Tent **36,** *47*
       Woolly Bear **106**
       Forest Tent *47*
Cattail *187*
Centipede 36, *48*

Cherry, Black **28**, *39*
Chipmunk, Eastern **33**, *43*
Chokeberry, Red **102**
Clubmoss *71*
Coltsfoot **125**, *135*
Cottongrass **228**
Cottontail, Eastern **127**, *136*
Cowbird, Brown-headed 21, **21**
Coyote, Eastern **116**, 120
Crabapple, American *91*
Cranberry 224
Creeper, Brown **35**, *46*
Cricket *115*
　　　Field **106**
　　　Snowy Tree 81, **87**
Crossbill, Red **148**,*151*
Damselfly, Black-winged **210**, *220*
Darner, Green 200, **210**
Dobsonfly, Eastern **210**
Dogwood 99
　　　Red Osier **103**
　　　Red-panicle **103**, *111*
Doll's Eyes **30**
Dove, Mourning **129**, *138*
Duck, Wood 196, **208**, *218*
Earthworm *142*
Earwig*142*
Elderberry, Common **205**, *215*
Ermine **122**, *136*
Fern
　　　Christmas **60**
　　　Cinnamon **161,** *166*
　　　Hay-scented *92*
　　　Interrupted *43*
　　　Ostrich**206**, *217*
　　　Royal **156**, **161**, *166*
　　　Sensitive *188*
Finch, Purple **105**
Fir, Balsam **59**, *69*
Fireweed **125**, *134*
Fisher **55**, **65**, *72*
Flea, Common **126**, *139*
Flicker, Northern **86**, *94*

Fly
　　　Crane **210**
　　　Goldenrod Gall 99, **106**
　　　Robber **106**
Flycatcher, Great Crested **35**, *46*
Foamflower **61**
Fox, Gray 81, **87**, *93*
Frog
　　　Green **180**
　　　Mink **180**, *191*
　　　Northern Leopard **104**
　　　Pickerel **180**, *191*
　　　Wood 21, **32**
Gentian, Closed **178**, *186*
Glowworms 171
Goldenrod 99, **104**
Goldfinch, American **105**
Goldthread **61**, *70*
Goose, Canada **128**, *137*
Goshawk, Northern *44*, **62**, *74*
Grass
　　　Bluejoint *216*
　　　Fowl Manna *188*
　　　Rattlesnake *188*
　　　Reed Canary *187*
Grasshopper **107**, *115*
Grosbeak, Rose-breasted **63**, *74*
Ground Cedar *71*
Grouse, Ruffed 53, **62**, *73*
Gull, Ring-billed **128**, *138*
Harrier, Northern 173, **179**, *189*
Harvester **181**, *193*
Hawk
　　　Broad-winged **34**
　　　Cooper's *44*
　　　Red-shouldered 196, **209**
　　　Red-tailed 118, **129**, *137*
　　　Sharp-shinned **34**, *44*
Hellebore, False **161**, *165*
Hemlock, Eastern 155, **160**, *165*
Hepatica, Sharp-lobed **31**, *42*
Heron
　　　Great Blue 171, **179**, *189*

Green *190*
Hobblebush *69*, **78**
Honeybee *139*
Hornet, Bald-faced *140*
Horsefly **211**
Horsetail, Rough **161**, *166*
Hummingbird, Ruby-throated
    86, *94*
Indian Pipe **60**, *71*
Jack-in-the-pulpit 20, **31**, *41*
Jewelweed
    Pale *186*
    Spotted 173, **178**, *186*
Joe-Pye-weed, Spotted **206**, *216*
Junco, Dark-eyed **105**
Katydid **36**
Kestrel, American **129**, *137*
Killdeer **128**, *138*
Kingfisher, Belted **208**, *219*
Kinglet
    Golden-crowned **63**, *74*
    Ruby-crowned **63**, *74*
Leafhopper **126**
Leatherleaf *185*
Lice, Book *141*
Lightning Bug 99, **106**
Lily, Canada **161**
Loon, Common **209**, *218*
Louse
    Body *141*
    Crab *141*
Maple
    Red 155, **160**, *165*
    Striped **29**, *40*
    Sugar **28**, *40*
Marsh Marigold **178**, *186*
Mayfly **211**
Meadowlark, Eastern 119, **129**
Meadow-Rue, Tall **178**
Merganser, Hooded 196, **208**, *218*
Midge **211**
Milkweed
    Common **104**, *111*
    Swamp 173, **178**

Millepedes **36**, *48*
Mink 201, **206**, *218*
Minnow, Cutlips *221*
Mites *141*
Moccasin-flower **60**, *70*
Mole
    Hairy-tailed **87**, *93*
    Star-nosed 197, **207**
Monarch 98, **107**, *113*
Mosquito 172, **172**
Moss
    Brook *216*
    Common Hairy Cap *71*
    Green Silk *43*
    Pin Cushion *71*
    Shining Club **60**
    Sphagnum 224, *232*
    Tree Club **61**
    Twisted Cord *135*
Moth
    Cecropia *47*
    Hummingbird **106**, *114*
    Io **36**
    Isabella Tiger *114*
    Luna **36**, *47*
Mourning Cloak **107**, *113*
Mouse
    Deer *71*, **104**
    Meadow Jumping **127**,
    136
    White-footed **87**
    Woodland Jumping **33**,
    44
Mud-dauber **107**
Mullein, Common **126**, *134*
Muskrat 174, **181**, *189*
Newt, Red Spotted **212**
Nuthatch
    Red-breasted **56, 63**, *75*
    White-breasted **63**, *75*
Oak
    Northern Red **29**, *39*
    White **29**, *39*
Opossum, Virginia *166*

Orchis, White-fringed **228**
Oriole, Baltimore **86**, *94*
Osprey **208**, *219*
Ovenbird 54, **63**
Owl
    Barred 55, **62**
    Eastern Screech **34**, *45*
    Great Horned **34**, *45*
    Northern Saw-whet
    62, *75*
    Snowy 120, **128**, *138*
Ox-Eye Daisy **125**, *133*
Partridgeberry **60**
Periodical Cicada **87**, *95*
Phoebe, Eastern **128**
Pine Marten **64**, *73*
Pine Sawyer 52, **64**, *76*
Pine
    Eastern White 51, **59**, *69*
    Red **148**
    Scotch **148**
Pitcher Plant 224, **226, 228**, *231*
Plantain, Common **125**, *134*
Pokeweed **125**, *134*
Porcupine 54, **54**, *72*
Praying Mantis **106**, *115*
Pussy Willow *215*
Queen-Anne's-Lace **126**, *133*
Question Mark *114*
Raccoon **207**, *217*
Raspberry *92*
Red Admiral **181**, *192*
Redstart, American 199, **209**
River Otter 201, **207**, *218*
Running Ground Pine **61**, *71*
Rush, Soft *188*
Salamander
    Northern Two-lined **212**
    Four-toed **180**, *190*
    Northern Dusky **212**
    Red-backed 52, **52**, *76*
    Spotted 22, **32**
    Spring **212**
Sandpiper

Solitary **179**, *190*
Spotted **179**, *190*
Sapsucker, Yellow-bellied **62**, *75*
Sassafras **102**
Sedge, Tussock *188*
Seed Bug, Western Conifer **148**
Serviceberry 80, **85**, *91*
Sheep Laurel *185*
Shrew
    Masked *112*
    Pygmy **104**, *112*
    Short-tailed *112*
    Smoky **104**
    Northern Water 197, **207**
Skullcap, Common **161**
Skunk Cabbage **161**
Skunk, Striped **87**, *93*
Smartweed *186*
Snake
    Brown **104**
    Eastern Milk 119, **127**
    Eastern Ribbon **180**, *192*
    Northern Water 199, **212**,
    220
    Red-bellied **32**, *47*
    Smooth Green **104**
Snow Flea 25, **36**, *48*
Snowshoe Hare **64**
Solomon's-seal, Hairy **30**
Sparrow
    Song 196, **209**
    White-throated **63**, *74*
Spicebush, Common **32**, *41*
Spider
    Black & Yellow Garden
    115
    Funnel Web *115*
    Goldenrod **107**, *115*
    Grass **107**
    Nursery-web *115*
    Wolf 23, **36**, *115*
Spring Azure **106**, *113*
Spring Peeper 21, 170, **180**
Spruce, Red **59**, *69*

Squirrel
    Gray **33**, *44*
    Red *72*
    Southern Flying 22, **33**
Squirrel-corn **30**
St. Johnwort, Common **178**
Starflower **60**
Steeplebush **102**, *111*
Sticktight **206**, *216*
Stinging Nettle **206**, *216*
Stinkbug, Green **126**, *140*
Stonefly **210**
Sumac, Staghorn **85**, *92*
Sundew 223, **228**, *231*
Swallow, Barn **128**, *138*
Swamp Candles **178**
Swift, Chimney **34**, *45*
Tamarack 155, **160**, *165*
Tanager, Scarlet 20, **35**, *46*
Teasel **125**, *134*
Thrasher, Brown **105**, *115*
Thrush
    Hermit *46*
    Swainson's *46*
    Wood 23, **35**, *46*
Tick, Deer *141*
Tiger Swallowtail **211**
Toad, American 170, **180**, *191*
Towhee, Eastern **86**, *93*
Treefrog, Gray 80, **80**
Treehopper **126**
Trillium
    Painted **31**, *42*
    Showy 20, **31**, *42*
Trout Lily **30**, *42*
Trout, Brook *220*
Turkey, Wild **34**
Turtle
    Bog **228**, *232*
    Common Snapping **212**, *219*
    Eastern Painted *192*
    Spotted *192*
    Wood **176**, *192*

Turtlehead **178**, *186*
Veery **35**
Viburnum **98**
Viceroy *113*
Vireo, Red-eyed **35**, *46*
Vole
    Meadow **104**, *112*
    Red-backed **33**, *43*
Wake Robin **41**, *42*
Walking Stick *139*
Warbler
    Blackburnian 80, **86**, *95*
    Black-throated Green 53, **63**, *74*
    Chestnut-sided 98, **105**
    Magnolia **78**, 80, **86**, *95*
    Yellow **86**, *94*
Wasp *139*
    Paper *139*
    Potter **107**
    Spider *140*
Water Lily, Sweet-scented *187*
Water Strider **211**
Waterthrush, Louisiana 225, **228**
Waxwing, Cedar **209**
Weasel
    Long-tailed *136*
    Short-tailed 120, **122**, *136*
Weevil, White Pine **126**, *140*
Whip-poor-will 81, **86**, *94*
White Tail Dragonfly **181**, *193*
White-tailed Deer **18**, 118, *135*
Wild Ginger **30**
Wild Leek **30**
Wild Mint *187*
Wild Oats **61**
Wild Raisin, Northern **103**, *111*
Wild Sarsarparilla **30**, *43*
Winterberry *185*
Witchhazel, Common 24, **32**, *41*
Wood Pewee, Eastern **86**
Wood Sorrel, Common **61**, *70*
Woodchuck **127**, *136*
Woodcock, American 98, **105**

Woodpecker
    Downy **35**
    Hairy **35**
    Pileated 24, **34**, *45*
Yarrow **125**, *133*
Yellowjacket *140*
Yellowthroat, Common 199, **209**

SPECIES LISTS

SPECIES LISTS

(Species in **boldface** type are included in this guide.)

TREES and SHRUBS

☐ **Speckled Alder** *Alnus rugosa*
☐ Apple *Malus sylvestris*
☐ Arbor Vitae *Thuja occidentalis*
☐ **Arrowwood** *Viburnum recognitum*
☐ **White Ash** *Fraxinus americana*
☐ **Bigtooth Aspen** *Populus grandidentata*
☐ **Quaking Aspen** *Populus tremuloides*
☐ Wild Azalea *Rhododendron roseum*
☐ Common Barberry *Berberis vulgaris*
☐ **American Basswood** *Tilia americana*
☐ **American Beech** *Fagus grandifolia*
☐ **Blue Beech** *Carpinus caroliniana*
☐ **Gray Birch** *Betula populifolia*
☐ Paper Birch *Betula papyrifera*
☐ **Yellow Birch** *Betula lutea*
☐ **American Black Currant** *Ribes americanum*
☐ Bladdernut *Staphylea trifolia*
☐ Blue Colonel *Cornus obliqua*
☐ **Highbush Blueberry** *Vaccinium corymbosum*
☐ Bog Rosemary *Andromeda glaucophylla*
☐ Common Buckthorn *Rhamnus cathartica*
☐ Glossy-leaved Buckthorn *Rhamnus frangula*
☐ Butternut *Juglans cinerea*
☐ **Buttonbush** *Cephalanthus occidentalis*
☐ Cassandra *Chamaedaphne calyculata*
☐ Eastern Red Cedar *Juniperus virginiana*
☐ **Black Cherry** *Prunus serotina*
☐ Choke Cherry *Prunus virginiana*
☐ Fire Cherry *Prunus penslyvanica*
☐ Rum Cherry *Prunus serotina*
☐ Sand Cherry *Prunus pumila*
☐ American Chestnut *Castanea dentata*
☐ Black Chokeberry *Aronia melanocarpa*
☐ **Red Chokeberry** *Pyrus arbutifolia*
☐ Cottonwood *Populus deltoides*

☐ **American Crabapple** *Pyrus coronaria*
☐ **Highbush Cranberry** *Viburnum trilobum*
☐ Daphne *Daphne mezereum*
☐ Deerberry *Vaccinium stamineum*
☐ Gray-stemmed Dogwood *Cornus racemosa*
☐ Green Osier Dogwood *Cornus alternifolia*
☐ **Red Osier Dogwood** *Cornus stolonifera*
☐ **Red-panicle Dogwood** *Cornus racemosa*
☐ Round-leaved Dogwood *Cornus rugosa*
☐ **Common Elderberry** *Sambucus canadensis*
☐ Red Elderberry *Sambucus pubens*
☐ American Elm *Ulmus americana*
☐ Slippery Elm *Ulmus rubra*
☐ **Balsam Fir** *Abies balsamea*
☐ Gooseberries and Currants *Ribes sp.*
☐ Hackberry *Celtis occidentalis*
☐ Hardhack *Spirea tomentosa*
☐ Hawthorns *Crataegus sp.*
☐ American Hazelnut *Corylus americana*
☐ Beaked Hazelnut *Corylus cornuta*
☐ **Eastern Hemlock** *Tsuga canadensis*
☐ Bitternut Hickory *Carya cordiformis*
☐ Pignut Hickory *Carya glabra*
☐ Shagbark Hickory *Carya ovata*
☐ **Hobblebush** *Viburnum alnifolium*
☐ Mountain Holly *Nemopanthus mucronata*
☐ Common Honeysuckle *Lonicera bella*
☐ Early Fly Honeysuckle *Lonicera canadensis*
☐ Mountain Fly Honeysuckle *Lonicera villosa*
☐ Swamp Fly Honeysuckle *Lonicera oblongifolia*

☐ Eastern Hophornbeam
 Ostraya virginiana
☐ American Hornbeam
 Carpinus caroliniana
☐ **Black Huckleberry**
 Gaylussacia baccata
☐ Dwarf Juniper *Juniperus communis*
☐ Labrador Tea *Ledum groenlandicum*
☐ Great Laurel *Rhododendron maximum*
☐ Mountain Laurel *Kalmia latifolia*
☐ Pale Laurel *Kalmia polifolia*
☐ **Sheep Laurel** *Kalmia augustifolia*
☐ **Leatherleaf** *Chamaedaphne calyculata*
☐ Mountain Maple *Acer spicatum*
☐ **Red Maple** *Acer rubrum*
☐ Silver Maple *Acer saccharinum*
☐ **Striped Maple** *Acer pennsylvanicum*
☐ **Sugar Maple** *Acer saccharum*
☐ Broad-leaved Meadowsweet
 Spirea latifolia
☐ American Mountain Ash
 Sorbus americana
☐ Nannyberry *Viburnum lentago*
☐ Nine-bark *Physocarpus opulifolius*
☐ **Northern Red Oak** *Quercus rubra*
☐ **White Oak** *Quercus alba*
☐ **Eastern White Pine**
 Pinus strobus
☐ Northern Scrub Pine
 Pinus banksiana
☐ Pitch Pine *Pinus rigida*
☐ **Red Pine** *Pinus resinosa*
☐ **Scotch Pine** *Pinus sylvestris*
☐ Canada Plum, *Prunus nigra*
☐ Balsam Poplar, *Populus balsamifera*
☐ Rhodora *Rhododendron canadense*
☐ Multiflora Rose *Rosa multiflora*
☐ Pasture Rose *Rosa carolina*
☐ Prickly Rose *Rosa acicularis*
☐ Swamp Rose *Rosa palustris*
☐ Sarsaparilla, Bristly
 Aralia hispida
☐ **Sassafras** *Sassafras albidum*
☐ **Serviceberry** *Amelanchier laevis*
☐ Wild Snowberry Bush
 Symphoricarpos racemosus
☐ **Common Spicebush**
 Lindera benzoin
☐ American Spikenard
 Aralia racemosa
☐ Black Spruce *Picea mariana*

☐ **Red Spruce** *Picea rubens*
☐ **Steeplebush** *Spirea tomentosa*
☐ **Staghorn Sumac** *Rhus typhina*
☐ Sweet-fern *Comptonia peregrina*
☐ Sweetgale *Myrica gale*
☐ **Tamarack** *Larix laricina*
☐ Maple-leaved Viburnum
 Viburnum acerifolium
☐ **Northern Wild Raisin**
 Viburnum cassinoides
☐ Black Willow *Salix nigra*
☐ **Pussy Willow** *Salix discolor*
☐ **Winterberry** *Ibex verticillata*
☐ **Common Witchhazel**
 Hamamelis virginiana
☐ American Yew *Taxus canadensis*

HERBACEOUS PLANTS

☐ Arrow-leaved Tearthumb
 Polygonum sagittatum
☐ Barren Strawberry *Waldsteinia fragarioides*
☐ **Bee Balm** *Monarda didyma*
☐ Bird's-eye Primrose *Primula mistassinica*
☐ Birdsfoot Trefoil *Lotus corniculatus*
☐ **Blackberry** *Rubus allegheniensis*
☐ Black-eyed Susan *Rudbeckia hirta*
☐ Bladder Campion *Silene cucubalus*
☐ Blind Gentian *Gentiana clausa*
☐ **Bloodroot** *Sanguinaria canadensis*
☐ **Blue Cohosh** *Caulophyllum thalictroides*
☐ Blue Curls *Trichostema dichotomum*
☐ **Blue Flag** *Iris versicolor*
☐ Blue Marsh Bellflower
 Campanula aparinoides
☐ Blue Vervain *Verbena hastata*
☐ Bluebell / Harebell *Campanula rotundifolia*
☐ Blue-eyed Grass *Sisyrinchium montanum*
☐ Bluets *Houstonia caerulea*
☐ **Bog Buckbean** *Menyanthes trifolata*
☐ **Boneset** *Eupatorium perfoliatum*
☐ Bouncing Bet *Saponaria officinalis*
☐ Brown Knapweed *Centaurea jacea*
☐ **Bull-Thistle** *Cirsium vulgare*
☐ **Bunchberry** *Cornus canadensis*
☐ **Burdock** *Arctium lappa*
☐ Butter-and-eggs *Linaria vulgaris*
☐ **Butterfly Weed** *Asclepias tuberosa*
☐ **Canada Anemone** *Anemone canadensis*
☐ Canada Goldenrod *Solidago canadensis*

☐ Canada Lily   *Lilium canadense*
☐ **Canada Mayflower** *Maianthemum canadense*
☐ Canada Violet   *Viola canadensis*
☐ Canadian Burnet   *Sanguisorba canadensis*
☐ Caraway   *Carum carvi*
☐ **Cardinal Flower**   *Lobelia cardinalis*
☐ **Carolina Spring Beauty**
   Claytonia caroliniana
☐ Carrion Flower   *Smilax herbacea*
☐ **Cattail**   *Typha latifolia*
☐ Chicory   *Cicorium intybus*
☐ Clammy Hedge Hyssop
   Gratiola neglecta
☐ Clintonia   *Clintonia borealis*
☐ **Closed Gentian**   *Gentiana andrewsii*
☐ **Coltsfoot**   *Tussilago farfara*
☐ Common Arrowhead
   Sagittaria latifolia
☐ Common Fleabane   *Erigeron philadelphicus*
☐ **Common Milkweed** *Asclepias syriaca*
☐ **Common Mullein**   *Verbascum thapsus*
☐ **Common Skullcap**   *Scutellaria nervosa*
☐ Common Speedwell *Veronica officinalis*
☐ **Common St. Johnswort**
   Hypericum perforatum
☐ **Common Wood Sorrel**
   Oxalis montana
☐ Cow Vetch   *Vicia cracca*
☐ Cow-lily   *Nuphar luteum*
☐ Creeping Bellflower *Campanula rapunculoides*
☐ Creeping Snowberry
   Gaultheria hispidula
☐ Crooked-stem Aster *Aster prenanthoides*
☐ Dandelion   *Taraxacum officinale*
☐ Deptford Pink   *Dianthus armeria*
☐ Devil's Paintbrush / Orange Hawkweed
   Hieracium aurantiacum
☐ Dewdrop   *Dalibarda repens*
☐ **Doll's Eyes**   *Actaea pachypoda*
☐ Dutchman's Breeches
   Dicentra cucullaria
☐ Dwarf Cinquefoil   *Potentilla canadensis*
☐ Dwarf Ginseng   *Panax trifolium*
☐ Dwarf Raspberry   *Rubus pubescens*
☐ Dwarf St. John's-wort
   Hypericum mutilum
☐ Early Saxifrage   *Saxifraga virginiensis*
☐ Elecampane   *Inula helenium*
☐ Evening Lychnis   *Lychnis alba*
☐ Evening Primrose   *Oenothera biennis*
☐ **False Hellebore**   *Veratrum viride*
☐ False Solomon's Seal
   Smilacina racemosa

☐ Fireweed   *Epilobium angustifolium*
☐ **Flat-leaved Bladderwort**
   Utricularia intermedia
☐ Flat-topped White Aster
   Aster umbellatus
☐ **Foamflower**   *Tiarella cordifolia*
☐ Fringed Gentian   *Gentiana crinita*
☐ Fringed Loosestrife *Lysimachia ciliata*
☐ Garlic Mustard   *Alliaria petiolata*
☐ Golden Alexanders *Zizia aurea*
☐ Golden Ragwort   *Senecio aureus*
☐ Golden Saxifrage   *Chrysosplenium americanum*
☐ **Goldenrod**   *Solidago sp.*
☐ **Goldthread**   *Coptis trifolia*
☐ Grass Pink   *Calopogon tuberosus*
☐ Grass-leaved Goldenrod
   Euthamia graminifolia
☐ Grass-of Parnassus *Parnassis glauca*
☐ Green Wood Orchis *Habenaria clavellata*
☐ Green-headed Coneflower
   Rudbeckia laciniata
☐ Hairy Solomon's Seal
   Polygonatum pubescens
☐ Harebell / Bluebell *Campanula rotundifolia*
☐ Heal-all   *Prunella vulgaris*
☐ Hedge Bineweed   *Convolvulus sepium*
☐ **Hepatica / Liverwort**
   Hepatica nobilis
☐ Hoary Alyssum   *Berteroa incana*
☐ Hog-peanut   *Amphicarpea bracteata*
☐ Indian Cucumber Root
   Medeola virginiana
☐ **Indian Pipe**   *Monotropa uniflora*
☐ Indian Tobacco   *Lobelia inflata*
☐ **Jack-in-the-pulpit**   *Arisaema atrorubens and A. stewardsonii*
☐ Jerusalem Artichoke *Helianthus tuberosus*
☐ Kaim's Lobelia   *Lobelia kaimii*
☐ Large-flowered Bellwort
   Uvularia grandiflora
☐ Large-leaved White Violet
   Viola cucullata
☐ **Leatherleaf**   *Chamaedaphne calyculata*
☐ Low Cudweed   *Gnaphalium uliginosum*
☐ Mad-dog Skullcap   *Scutellaria lateriflora*
☐ Marsh Bedstraw   *Galium palustre*
☐ Marsh Blue Violet   *Viola cucullata*
☐ Marsh Cinquefoil   *Potentilla palustris*
☐ **Marsh Marigold / Cowslip**
   Caltha palustris
☐ Marsh Skullcap   *Scutellaria galericulata*

☐ Marsh Speedwell   *Veronica scutellata*
☐ Marsh St. John's-wort
                  Triadenum virginicum
☐ Marsh Willow-herb *Epilobium palustre*
☐ Mayapple   *Podophyllum peltatum*
☐ Meadowsweet   *Spiraea latifolia*
☐ Miterwort / Bishop's Cap
                  Mitella diphylla
☐ **Moccasin-flower / Pink Lady Slipper**
                  Cypripedium acaule
☐ Mountain Sandwort *Arenaria groenlandica*
☐ Narrow-leaved Gentian
                  Gentiana linearis
☐ New York Aster   *Aster novi-belgii*
☐ Nodding Ladies' Tresses
                  Spiranthes cernua
☐ Northern White Violet
                  Viola pallens
☐ One-flowered Wintergreen
                  Moneses uniflora
☐ Oxalis Wood Sorrel *Oxalis acetosella*
☐ **Ox-Eye Daisy**   **Chrysanthemum**
                  leucanthemum
☐ **Painted Trillium** **Trillium undulatum**
☐ **Pale Jewelweed** **Impatiens pallida**
☐ Pale St. John's-wort *Hypericum ellipticum*
☐ **Partridgeberry**   **Mitchella repens**
☐ Pasture Rose   *Rosa carolina*
☐ Pearly Everlasting *Anaphalis margaritacea*
☐ Pennsylvania Bitter Crest
            Cardamine pensylvanica
☐ Pickerelweed   *Pontederia cordata*
☐ Pipsissewa   *Chimaphila umbellata*
☐ **Pitcher Plant**   **Sarracinia purpurea**
☐ **Plantain**   **Plantago major**
☐ Poison Ivy   *Toxicodendron radicans*
☐ **Pokeweed**   **Phytolacca americana**
☐ Pondweeds   *Potamogeton spp.*
☐ Purple Fringed Orchid
                Habenaria fimbriata
☐ Purple Loosestrife *Lythrum salicaria*
☐ Purple-flowering Raspberry
                Rubus odoratus
☐ Purple-stemmed Aster
                Aster puniceus
☐ Pussytoes   *Antennaria spp.*
☐ **Queen-Anne's-Lace**
                Daucus carota
☐ Red Baneberry   *Actaea spicata*
☐ **Red Raspberry**   **Rubus idaeus**
☐ Rose Pogonia / Snake-mouth
            Pogonia ophioglossoides
☐ Rough Cinquefoil *Potentilla norvegica*
☐ Rough-fruited Cinquefoil
                Potentilla recta

☐ Rough-stemmed Goldenrod
                Solidago rugosa
☐ Round-leaved Pyrola
                Pyrola rotundifolia
☐ **Sharp-lobed Hepatica**
                Hepatica acutiloba
☐ Sheep Sorrel   *Rumex acetosella*
☐ Shinleaf   *Pyrola elliptica*
☐ **Showy Trillium** **Trillium grandiflorum**
☐ Smaller Purple Fringed Orchis
                Habenaria psycodes
☐ **Smartweed**   **Polygonum spp.**
☐ **Solomon's-seal** **Polygonatum biflorum**
☐ Spikenard   *Aralia racemosa*
☐ **Spotted Jewelweed Impatiens capensis**
☐ Spotted Joe-Pye Weed
            Eupatorium maculatum
☐ Spotted Knapweed *Centaurea maculosa*
☐ Spreading Dogbane *Apocynum*
                androsaemifolium
☐ **Squirrel-corn**   **Dicentra canadensis**
☐ **Starflower**   **Trientalis borealis**
☐ Star-flowered Solomon's Seal
                Smilacina stellata
☐ Stinging Nettles *Urtica dioica*
☐ **Sundew**   **Drosera rotundifolia**
                  intermedia
☐ Sundrops   *Oenothera fruticosa*
☐ Swamp Buttercup *Ranunculus*
                septentrionalis
☐ **Swamp Candles** **Lysimachia terrestris**
☐ **Swamp Milkweed Asclepias incarnata**
☐ Swamp Saxifrage *Saxifraga pensylvanica*
☐ Sweet-scented Bedstraw
                Galium triflorum
☐ Tall Buttercup   *Ranunculus acris*
☐ **Tall Meadow Rue** **Thalictrum polygamum**
☐ **Teasel**   **Dipsacus sylvestris**
☐ Trailing Arbutus *Epigaea repens*
☐ **Trout Lily**   **Erythronium**
                americanum
☐ True Forget-me-not *Myosotis scorpioides*
☐ **Turtlehead**   **Chelone glabra**
☐ Twinflower   *Linnaea borealis*
☐ Twisted-stalk Rose / Rosybells
                Streptopus roseus
☐ Two-leaved Toothwort
                Dentaria diphylla
☐ Viper's Bugloss *Echium vulgare*
☐ Virginia Creeper *Parthenocissus*
                quinquefolia
☐ Virginia Waterleaf *Hydrophyllum*
                virginianum
☐ Virgin's Bower *Clematis virginiana*
☐ **Wake Robin**   **Trillium erectum**

☐ Water Arum *Calla palustris*
☐ Water Avens *Geum rivale*
☐ Water Horehound *Lycopus americanus*
☐ **Water Lily, Sweet-scented**
    Nymphaea odorata
☐ Water Parsnip *Sium suave*
☐ Water Purslane *Ludwigia paliustris*
☐ White Bog Orchis *Habenaria dilatata*
☐ **White-fringed Orchis**
    Habenaria blephariglottis
☐ Whorled Aster *Aster acuminatus*
☐ Wild Columbine *Aquilegia canadensis*
☐ **Wild Ginger** **Asarum canadense**
☐ **Wild Leek** **Allium tricoccum**
☐ **Wild Mint** **Mentha arvensis**
☐ **Wild Oat** **Uvularia sessilifolia**
☐ Wild Parsnip *Pastinaca sativa*
☐ **Wild Sarsarparilla** **Aralia nudicaulis**
☐ Wild Strawberry *Fragaria virginiana*
☐ Wintergreen *Gaultheria procumbens*
☐ Wood Anemone *Anemone quinquefolia*
☐ Wood Horsetail *Equisetum sylvaticum*
☐ **Yarrow or Milfoil** **Achillea millefolium**
☐ Yellow Goatsbeard *Tragopogon pratensis*
☐ Yellow Mountain Saxifrage
    Saxifraga aizoides
☐ Yellow Pond Lily *Nuphar variegatum*
☐ Yellow Rocket *Barbarea vulgaris*

MOSSES and FERNS

MOSSES, ETC.

☐ **Brook Moss** **Fontinalis antipyretica**
☐ Broom Moss *Dicranum scoparium*
☐ **Common Hairy Cap Moss**
    Polytrichum commune
☐ Exquisite Feather Moss
    Calliergon spp.
☐ Flat Tufted Feather Moss
    Hypnum imponens
☐ **Green Silk Moss** **Brachythecium**
    oxycladon
☐ Marchantia Moss *Marchantia polymorpha*
☐ **Sphagnum Moss** **Sphagnum sp.**
☐ **Pin Cushion Moss** **Leucobryum glaucum**
☐ Pointed Bog Feather Moss
    Calliergonella cuspidata
☐ Ribbed Bog Moss *Aulocomium palustre*
☐ Snake Liverwort *Conocephalum conicum*
☐ **Three-lobed Bazzania**
    Bazzania trilobata
☐ Tree Moss *Climacium dendroides*
☐ **Twisted Cord Moss** *Funaria hygrometrica*

FERNS, ETC.

☐ Bracken Fern *Pteridium aquilinum*
☐ Bulblet Fern *Cystopteris bulbifera*
☐ **Christmas Fern** **Polystichum**
    arcrostichoides
☐ **Cinnamon Fern** **Osmunda cinnamomea**
☐ **Clubmoss** **Lycopodium sp**
☐ Common Fragile Fern
    Cystopteris fragilis
☐ Common Wood Fern
    Dryopteris intermedia
☐ Cut-leaved Grape Fern
    Botrychium dissectum
☐ Field Horsetail *Equisetum arvense*
☐ **Ground Cedar** **Lycopodium**
    tristachyum
☐ **Hay-scented Fern** **Dennstaedtia**
    punctilobula
☐ **Interrupted Fern** **Osmunda claytoniana**
☐ Lady Fern *Athyrium asplenioides*
☐ Long Beech Fern *Thelypteris phegopteris*
☐ Maidenhair Fern *Adiantum pedatum*
☐ **Ostrich Fern** **Matteuccia**
    struthiopteris
☐ Polypody Fern *Polypodium virginianum*
☐ Rattlesnake Fern *Botrychium virginianum*
☐ **Royal Fern** **Osmunda regalis**
☐ **Running Ground Pine**
    Lycopodium
    flabelliforme
☐ **Sensitive Fern** **Onoclea sensibilis**
☐ **Shining Clubmoss** **Lycopodium**
    lucidulum
☐ Silvery Spleenwort *Athyrium thelypterioides*
☐ Staghorn Clubmoss *Lycopodium clavatum*
☐ **Tree Clubmoss** **Lycopodium obscurum**
☐ **Rough Horsetail** **Equisetum sylvaticum**

GRASSES, RUSHES, AND SEDGES

☐ Cattail   *Typha latifolia*
☐ Barnyard Grass   *Echinochioa crus-galli*
☐ **Bluejoint Grass**   **Calamagrostis canadensis**
☐ Canada Blue Grass   *Poa compressa*
☐ Drooping Woodreed*Cinna latifolia*
☐ **Fowl Mannagrass**   **Glyceria striata**
☐ Kentucky Blue Grass
                                Poa pratensis
☐ Low Spear Grass   *Poa annua*
☐ Milletgrass   *Milium effusum*
☐ Northern Panic Grass
                                Panicum boreale
☐ Old-pasture Bluegrass
                                Poa saltuensis
☐ Orchard Grass   *Dactylis glomerata*
☐ Panic Grass   *Panicum acruminatum*
☐ Poverty-grass   *Danthonia spicata*
☐ **Rattlesnake Grass** **Glyceria canadensis**
☐ Redtop   *Agrostis gignantea*
☐ **Reed Canary Grass** **Phalaris arundinacea**

☐ Rice cut-grass   *Leersia oryzoides*
☐ Slender Mannagrass*Glyceria melicaria*
☐ Sweet Vernal Grass
                                Anthoxanthum odoratum
☐ Ticklegrass   *Agrostis hiemalis*
☐ Timothy   *Phleum pratense*
☐ Tufted Hairgrass   *Deschampsia cespitosa*
☐ **Soft Rush**   **Juncus effusus**
☐ Path Rush   *Juncus tenuis*
☐ Toad Rush   *Juncus bufonius*
☐ **Sedge**   **Carex sp.**
☐ Alpine Cottongrass   *Eriophorum alpinum*
☐ Bulrush   *Scirpus microcarpus*
☐ **Cottongrass**   **Eriophorum viridicarinatum**
☐ Northern Bulrush   *Scirpus atrocinctus*
☐ Plantain   *Carex plantaginea*
☐ Spikerush   *Eleocharis obtusa*
☐ Tawny Cottongrass   *Eriophorum virginicum*
☐ Three-way Sedge   *Dulichium arundinaceum*
☐ **Tussock Sedge**   **Carex stricta**
☐ White Beakrush   *Rhynchospora alba*
☐ Sweetflag   *Acorus calamus*

MAMMALS

☐ Big Brown Bat   *Eptesicus fuscus*
☐ Eastern Pipistrelle   *Pipistrellus subflavus*
☐ Hoary Bat   *Lasiurus cinereus*
☐ **Indiana Bat**   **Myotis sodalis**
☐ Keen's Myotis   *Myotis keenii*
☐ **Little Brown Bat**   **Myotis lucifugus**
☐ Red Bat   *Lasiurus borealis*
☐ Silver-haired Bat   *Lasionycteris noctivagans*
☐ Small-footed Bat   *Myotis leibii*
☐ **Bear, Black**   *Ursus americanus*
☐ **Beaver**   *Castor canadensis*
☐ **Bobcat**   *Felis rufus*
☐ **Chipmunk, Eastern** *Tamias striatus*
☐ **Cottontail, Eastern** *Sylvilagus floridanus*
☐ **Coyote, Eastern**   *Canis latrans*
☐ **Deer, White-tailed** *Odocoileus virginianus*
☐ **Ermine**   *Mustela erminea*
☐ **Fisher**   *Martes pennanti*
☐ **Gray Fox**   **Urocyon cinereoargenteus**
☐ Red Fox   *Vulpes vulpes*
☐ **Snowshoe Hare**   **Lepus americanus**
☐ Northern Bog Lemming
                                Synaptomys borealis
☐ Southern Bog Lemming
                                Synaptomys cooperi
☐ **Mink**   **Mustela vison**
☐ **Hairy-tailed Mole** **Parascalops breweri**
☐ **Star-nosed Mole**   **Condylura cristata**
☐ Moose   *Alces alces*
☐ **Deer Mouse**   **Peromyscus maniculatus**
☐ **Meadow Jumping Mouse**
                                Zapus hudsonicus
☐ **White-footed Mouse**
                                Peromyscus leucopis
☐ **Woodland Jumping Mouse**
                                Napaeozapus insignis
☐ **Muskrat**   **Ondatra zibethicus**
☐ **Opossum, Virginia** *Didelphis virginiana*
☐ **Pine Marten**   **Martes americana**
☐ **Porcupine**   **Erethizon dorsatum**
☐ **Raccoon**   **Procyon lotor**
☐ **River Otter**   **Lutra canadensis**
☐ Long-tailed Shrew   *Sorex dispar*
☐ **Masked Shrew**   **Sorex cinereus**
☐ **Pygmy Shrew**   **Sorex hoyi**
☐ **Short-tailed Shrew** **Blarina brevicauda**
☐ **Smoky Shrew**   **Sorex fumeus**
☐ Northern Water Shrew
                                Sorex palustris
☐ **Striped Skunk**   **Mephitis mephitis**
☐ **Gray Squirrel**   **Sciurus carolinensis**

☐ Northern Flying Squirrel
Glaucomys sabrinus
☐ **Red Squirrel** *Tamiasciurus hudsonicus*
☐ **Southern Flying Squirrel**
Glaucomys volans
☐ **Meadow Vole** *Microtus pennsylvanicus*
☐ **Red-backed Vole** *Clethrionomys gapperi*
☐ Rock Vole *Microtus chrotorrhinus*
☐ Woodland Vole *Microtus pinetorum*
☐ **Weasel** *Mustela frenata*
☐ **Woodchuck** *Marmota monax*

BIRDS

☐ **American Bittern** *Botaurus lentiginosus*
☐ **Red-winged Blackbird**
Agelaius phoeniceus
☐ **Eastern Bluebird** *Sialis sialis*
☐ **Bobolink** *Dolichonyx Oryzivorus*
☐ Brant *Branta bernicla*
☐ Bufflehead *Bucephala albeola*
☐ **Indigo Bunting** *Passerina Cyanea*
☐ Snow Bunting *Plectrophenax nivalis*
☐ Canvasback *Aythya valisineria*
☐ Cardinal *Cardinalis cardinalis*
☐ **Gray Catbird** *Dumetella carolinensis*
☐ Black-capped Chickadee
Parus atricapillus
☐ American Coot *Fulica americana*
☐ Double-crested Cormorant
Phalacrocorax auritus
☐ **Brown-headed Cowbird**
Molothrus ater
☐ **Brown Creeper** *Certhia familiaris*
☐ **Red Crossbill** *Loxia curvirostra*
☐ White-winged Crossbill
Loxia leucoptera
☐ American Crow *Corvus brachyrhynchos*
☐ Black-billed Cuckoo
Coccyzus erythropthalmus
☐ **Mourning Dove** *Zenaida macroura*
☐ Rock Dove (pigeon) *Columba livia*
☐ Black Duck *Anas rubripes*
☐ Ring-necked Duck *Aythya collaris*
☐ Ruddy Duck *Oxyura jamaicensis*
☐ **Wood Duck** *Aix sponsa*
☐ Bald Eagle *Haliaeetus leucocephalus*
☐ Golden Eagle *Aquila chrysaetos*
☐ Cattle Egret *Bubulcus ibis*
☐ Common Eider *Somateria mollissima*
☐ Peregrine Falcon *Falco peregrinus*

☐ House Finch *Carpodacus mexicanus*
☐ **Purple Finch** *Carpodacus purpureus*
☐ **Northern Flicker** *Colaptes auratus*
☐ **Great Crested Flycatcher**
Myiarchus crinitus
☐ Willow Flycatcher *Empidonax traillii*
☐ Common Goldeneye
Bucephala clangula
☐ **American Goldfinch**
Carduelis tristis
☐ **Canada Goose** *Branta canadensis*
☐ Snow Goose *Chen caerulescens*
☐ **Northern Goshawk** *Accipiter gentilis*
☐ Common Grackle *Quiscalus quiscula*
☐ Pied-billed Grebe *Podilymbus podiceps*
☐ Evening Grosbeak *Coccothraustes vespertinus*
☐ Pine Grosbeak *Pinicola enucleator*
☐ **Rose-breasted Grosbeak**
Pheucticus ludovicianus
☐ **Ruffed Grouse** *Bonasa umbellus*
☐ Spruce Grouse *Dendragapus canadensis*
☐ **Ring-billed Gull** *Larus delawarensis*
☐ Gyrfalcon *Falco rusticolus*
☐ **Northern Harrier** *Circus cyaneus*
☐ **Broad-winged Hawk**
Buteo platypterus
☐ **Cooper's Hawk** *Accipiter cooperii*
☐ **Red-shouldered Hawk**
Buteo lineatus
☐ **Red-tailed Hawk** *Buteo jamaicensis*
☐ Rough-legged Hawk
Buteo lagopus
☐ **Sharp-shinned Hawk**
Accipiter striatus
☐ **Great Blue Heron** *Ardea herodias*
☐ **Green Heron**
Butorides striatus
☐ **Ruby-throated Hummingbird**
Archilochus colubris
☐ Glossy Ibis *Plegadis falcinellus*
☐ Blue Jay *Cyanocitta cristata*
☐ Gray Jay *Perisoreus canadensis*
☐ **Dark-eyed Junco** *Junco hyemalis*
☐ **American Kestrel** *Falco sparverius*
☐ **Killdeer** *Charadrius vociferus*
☐ Eastern Kingbird *Tyrannus tyrannus*
☐ **Belted Kingfisher** *Ceryle alcyon*
☐ **Golden-crowned Kinglet**
Regulus satrapa
☐ **Ruby-crowned Kinglet**
Regulus calendula
☐ Horned Lark *Eremophila alpestris*
☐ Lapland Longspur *Calcarius lapponicus*

☐ **Common Loon** *Gavia immer*
☐ Mallard *Anas platyrhynchos*
☐ **Eastern Meadowlark**
  Sturnella magna
☐ **Hooded Merganser** *Lophodytes cucullatus*
☐ Northern Mockingbird
  Mimus polyglottos
☐ Common Moorhen *Gallinula chloropus*
☐ Black-crowned Night-Heron
  Nycticorax nycticorax
☐ **Red-breasted Nuthatch**
  Sitta canadensis
☐ **White-breasted Nuthatch**
  Sitta carolinensis
☐ **Baltimore Oriole** *Icterus galbula*
☐ **Osprey** *Pandion haliaetus*
☐ **Ovenbird** *Seiurus aurocapillus*
☐ **Barred Owl** *Strix varia*
☐ Boreal Owl *Aegolius funereus*
☐ **Eastern Screech Owl**
  Otus asio
☐ Great Gray Owl *Strix nebulosa*
☐ **Great Horned Owl** *Bubo virginanus*
☐ Long-eared Owl *Asio otus*
☐ Northern Hawk Owl
  Surnia ulula
☐ **Northern Saw-whet Owl**
  Aegolius acadicus
☐ Short-eared Owl *Asio flammeus*
☐ **Snowy Owl** *Nyctea scandiaca*
☐ Ring-necked Pheasant
  Phasianus colchicus
☐ **Eastern Phoebe** *Sayornis phoebe*
☐ Northern Pintail *Anas acuta*
☐ Virginia Rail *Rallus limicola*
☐ Common Raven *Corvus corax*
☐ Redhead *Aythya americana*
☐ Common Redpoll *Carduelis flammea*
☐ **American Redstart** *Setophaga ruticilla*
☐ American Robin *Turdus migratorius*
☐ **Solitary Sandpiper** *Tringa solitaria*
☐ **Spotted Sandpiper** *Actitis macularia*
☐ **Yellow-bellied Sapsucker**
  Sphyrapicus varius
☐ Northern Shoveler *Anas clypeata*
☐ Northern Shrike *Lanius excubitor*
☐ Pine Siskin *Carduelis pinus*
☐ Chipping Sparrow *Spizella passerina*
☐ House Sparrow *Passer domesticus*
☐ **Song Sparrow** *Melospiza melodia*
☐ **White-throated Sparrow**
  Zonotrichia albicollis
☐ European Starling *Sturnus vulgaris*
☐ Bank Swallow *Riparia riparia*
☐ **Barn Swallow** *Hirundo rustica*

☐ Tundra Swan *Olor columbianus*
☐ **Chimney Swift** *Chaetura pelagica*
☐ **Scarlet Tanager** *Piranga olivacea*
☐ Blue-winged Teal *Anas discors*
☐ Green-winged Teal *Anas crecca*
☐ Common Tern *Sterna hirundo*
☐ **Brown Thrasher** *Toxostoma rufum*
☐ **Hermit Thrush** *Catharus guttatus*
☐ **Swainson's Thrush** *Catharus ustulatus*
☐ **Wood Thrush** *Hylocichla mustelina*
☐ Tufted Titmouse *Parus bicolor*
☐ **Eastern Towhee** *Pipilo*
  erythrophthalmus
☐ **Wild Turkey** *Meleagris gallopavo*
☐ **Veery** *Catharus fuscescens*
☐ **Red-eyed Vireo** *Vireo olivaceus*
☐ Turkey Vulture *Cathartes aura*
☐ Black and White Warbler
  Mniotilta varia
☐ **Blackburnian Warbler**
  Dendroica fusca
☐ Black-throated Blue Warbler
  Dendroica caerulescens
☐ **Black-throated Green Warbler**
  Dendroica virens
☐ **Chestnut-sided Warbler**
  Dendroica pensylvanica
☐ **Magnolia Warbler** *Dendroica magnolia*
☐ **Yellow Warbler** *Dendroica petechia*
☐ **Louisiana Waterthrush**
  Seiurus motacilla
☐ **Cedar Waxwing** *Bombycilla cedrorum*
☐ **Whip-poor-will** *Caprimulgus vociferus*
☐ American Wigeon *Anas americana*
☐ **American Woodcock**
  Scolopax minor
☐ Black-backed Woodpecker
  Picoides arcticus
☐ **Downy Woodpecker**
  Picoides pubescens
☐ **Hairy Woodpecker** *Picoides villosus*
☐ **Pileated Woodpecker**
  Dryocopus pileatus
☐ Red-headed Woodpecker
  Melanerpes
  erythrocephalus
☐ **Eastern Wood Pewee**
  Contopus virens
☐ House Wren *Troglodytes aedon*
☐ **Common Yellowthroat**
  Geothlypis trichas

AMPHIBIANS AND REPTILES

☐ Bullfrog	*Rana catesbeiana*
☐ Green Frog	*Rana clamitans melanota*
☐ Mink Frog	*Rana septentrionalis*
☐ Northern Leopard Frog	*Rana pipiens*
☐ Pickerel Frog	*Rana palustris*
☐ Wood Frog	*Rana sylvatica*
☐ Mudpuppy	*Necturus maculosis*
☐ Red-spotted Newt	*Notopthalamus viridescens*
☐ Spring Peeper	*Pseudacris crucifer*
☐ Four-toed Salamander	*Hemidactylum scutatum*
☐ Jefferson's Salamander	*Ambystoma jeffersonianum*
☐ Mountain Dusky Salamander	*Desmognathus ochrophaeus*
☐ Northern Dusky Salamander	*Desmognathus fuscus*
☐ Red-backed Salamander	*Plethodon cinereus*
☐ Spotted Salamander	*Ambystoma maculatum*
☐ Spring Salamander	*Gyrinophilus porphyriticus*
☐ Northern Two-lined Salamander	*Eurycea bislineata*
☐ Eastern Garter Snake	*Thamnophis sirtalis*
☐ Eastern Milk Snake	*Lampropeltis triangulum triangulum*
☐ Eastern Ribbon Snake	*Thamnophis sauritis sauritis*
☐ Smooth Green Snake	*Opheodryas vernalis vernalis*
☐ Maritime Garter Snake	*Thamnophis sirtalis pallidula*
☐ Red-bellied Snake	*Storeria occipitomaculata occipitomaculata*
☐ Northern Ringneck Snake	*Diadophis punctatus edwardsi*
☐ Northern Water Snake	*Nerodia sipedon sipedon*
☐ Brown Snake	*Storeria dekayi dekayi*
☐ American Toad	*Bufo americanus*
☐ Gray Treefrog	*Hyla versicolor*
☐ Blanding's Turtle	*Emydoidea blandingi*
☐ Bog Turtle	*Clemmys muhlenbergi*
☐ Common Snapping Turtle	*Chelydra serpentina*
☐ Eastern Painted Turtle	*Chrysemys picta picta*
☐ Midland Painted Turtle	*Chrysemys picta marginata*
☐ Spotted Turtle	*Clemmys guttata*
☐ Wood Turtle	*Clemmys insculpta*

INSECTS

(ORDERS)

☐ Snow Flea	*Collembola*
☐ Mayflies	*Ephemeroptera*
☐ Green Darner	*Odonata*
☐ White Tail Dragonfly	*Odonata*
☐ Damselfly	*Odonata*
☐ Grasshoppers	*Orthoptera*
☐ Crickets	*Orthoptera*
☐ Katydid	*Orthoptera*
☐ Snowy Tree Cricket	*Orthoptera*
☐ Mantids	*Mantodea*
☐ Walking Sticks	*Mantodea*
☐ Stoneflies	*Plecoptera*
☐ Earwigs	*Dermaptera*
☐ Booklice	*Psocoptera*
☐ Body Louse	*Mallopaga*
☐ Crab Louse	*Mallopaga*
☐ Giant Water Bug	*Hemiptera*
☐ Water Boatmen	*Hemiptera*
☐ Backswimmers	*Hemiptera*
☐ Water Striders	*Hemiptera*
☐ Ambush Bugs	*Hemiptera*
☐ Assasin Bugs	*Hemiptera*
☐ Leaf Bugs	*Hemiptera*
☐ Stink Bugs	*Hemiptera*
☐ Cicadas	*Homoptera*
☐ Treehoppers	*Homoptera*
☐ Leafhoppers	*Homoptera*
☐ Spittlebugs	*Homoptera*
☐ Adhids	*Homoptera*

☐ Woolly Aphids   *Homoptera*
☐ **Dobsonflies**   *Neuroptera*
☐ **Antlions**   *Neuroptera*
☐ Lacewings   *Neuroptera*
☐ **Tiger Beetles**   *Coleoptera*
☐ **Ground Beetles**   *Coleoptera*
☐ **Predaceous Diving Beetle**
                    Coleoptera
☐ **Whirligig Beetles** *Coleoptera*
☐ Water Beetles   *Coleoptera*
☐ **Carrion Beetles**   *Coleoptera*
☐ Rove Beetles   *Coleoptera*
☐ Soldier Beetles   *Coleoptera*
☐ **Fireflies**   *Coleoptera*
☐ Click Beetles   *Coleoptera*
☐ Borers   *Coleoptera*
☐ Bark Beetles   *Coleoptera*
☐ **Ladybird Beetles**   *Coleoptera*
☐ Darkling Beetles   *Coleoptera*
☐ Stag Beetles   *Coleoptera*
☐ Scarab Beetles   *Coleoptera*
☐ **Sawyers**   *Coleoptera*
☐ **Leaf Beetles**   *Coleoptera*
☐ **Weevils**   *Coleoptera*
☐ Twisted-wing Parasites
                    Strepsiptera
☐ Scorpionflies & Kin
                    Mecoptera
☐ **Caddisflies**   *Trichoptera*
☐ **Mourning Cloak**   *Lepidoptera*
☐ **Monarch**   *Lepidoptera*
☐ **Tiger Swallowtail** *Lepidoptera*
☐ Cabbage and Alfalfa Butterflies
                    Lepidoptera
☐ **American Painted Lady**
                    Lepidoptera
☐ **Spring Azure**   *Lepidoptera*
☐ **Banded Purple**   *Lepidoptera*
☐ **Buckeye**   *Lepidoptera*
☐ White Admiral   *Lepidoptera*
☐ **Red Admiral**   *Lepidoptera*
☐ **Luna Moth**   *Lepidoptera*
☐ **Cecropia Moth**   *Lepidoptera*
☐ **Isabella Tiger Moth**
                    Lepidoptera
☐ **Hummingbird Moth**
                    Lepidoptera
☐ **Io Moth**   *Lepidoptera*
☐ **Tent Caterpillars** *Lepidoptera*
☐ Fall Webworm   *Lepidoptera*
☐ Gypsy Moth   *Lepidoptera*
☐ **Crane Flies**   *Diptera*
☐ Mosquitoes   *Diptera*
☐ **Midges**   *Diptera*
☐ **Black Flies**   *Diptera*

☐ **Gall Gnats**   *Diptera*
☐ **Horse and Deer Flies**
                    Diptera
☐ **Robber Flies**   *Diptera*
☐ Bee Flies   *Diptera*
☐ Blow Flies   *Diptera*
☐ **Fleas**   *Siphonaptera*
☐ Sawflies   *Hymenoptera*
☐ **Ichneumonids**   *Hymenoptera*
☐ Gall Wasps   *Hymenoptera*
☐ **Ants**   *Hymenoptera*
☐ **Spider Wasps**   *Hymenoptera*
☐ **Paper Wasps**   *Hymenoptera*
☐ **Potter Wasps**   *Hymenoptera*
☐ **Mud-dauber**   *Hymenoptera*
☐ **Yellowjackets and Hornets**
                    Hymenoptera
☐ **Carpenter Bees**   *Hymenoptera*
☐ **Bumble Bees**   *Hymenoptera*
☐ **Honey Bees**   *Hymenoptera*

THE WRITERS

DESIGNER, ILLUSTRATOR, EDITOR

Robert McNamara - Creator of color illustrations, paintings, and drawings. Contributing photographer. Designer of book layout and finder system. Editor of material contributed by writing team.

Bob is an artist, photographer, and writer who shares a piece of the Tug Hill second generation wilderness with many of the species that inspire his work. His formal education was at the College of Environmental Science and Forestry where he received Bachelor of Science in Environmental Studies and Bachelor of Landscape Architecture degrees.

His first career in Landscape Architecture evolved into a consulting business in Environmental Interpretation and Fine Art. His credentials in art include membership in the Society of Animal Artists, and inclusion in many world class wildlife art exhibits, shows, and publications. His work has appeared many times in *Wildlife Art* magazine, the pre-eminent magazine of the genre, and he was a contributing artist and writer for a recently published book titled *The Best of Wildlife Art*, published by North Light Books. His writings have appeared in *Adirondack Life, The Conservationist*, and *Ranger Rick*.

He brings to the project the ability to pull together and manage the writings of a diverse group of professionals and present them in a way that will engage the amateur naturalist.

CONTRIBUTING WRITERS

The contributing writers to the project possess not only a high level of technical expertise combined with great writing skills, but they also have either spent a good part of their lives on Tug Hill or have specialized in some aspect of Tug Hill natural history.

John Cecil - Contributing writer on geology and surface drainage patterns of the Hill. Contributing writer of poetry.

John is a retired professor of Geology at Jefferson Community College

(JCC) in Watertown, N.Y. He taught at JCC from 1967-1992. John received Bachelors and Masters degrees in Science Education with an emphasis in geology from the State University of New York at Cortland (SUNY Cortland). Prior to coming to JCC, he taught geology at the high school level, and at the SUNY Oneonta.

John's articles have appeared in the *Journal of Geologic Education* and the *Black River Review*. He wrote a study guide of *Jefferson County Fossils* for the Jefferson County Historical Society. He also wrote a *Lab Manual for Physical and Historical Geology*.

Until recently John and his family lived in Adams Center, on the northwest side of Tug Hill. Since retirement he has concentrated on photographing wildlife and landscapes; much of his work is on Tug Hill. He also writes prose and poetry inspired by his experiences in his Tug Hill back yard.

Lee B. Chamberlaine - Contributing writer on birds, mammals, insects, trees, herbaceous plants, plant communities, and wetlands.

Lee retired from the New York State Department of Environmental Conservation in 1991, having worked as a Wildlife Biologist in Region 6 (Watertown office) for over 25 years. A major part of Tug Hill fell within his jurisdiction at work, where he studied and managed wetlands and plant and animal communities on State owned lands. Lee graduated from The SUNY College of Forestry in 1963 with a Bachelors degree in Land Management. He lives on the western edge of the Hill.

He is active in the Adirondack Conservancy, the Onondaga Chapter of the National Audubon Society, The Nature Conservancy, The Wildlife Society, the Society of American Foresters, and many other conservation groups. His writings have been published in *The Conservationist* magazine. He contributed work to *Birds of New York* by John Bull. He is editor of the *Kingbird* for the New York State Federation of Bird Clubs. He is well known as an expert in many aspects of Tug Hill ecology, especially areas related to birds.

Peter Gaskin - Contributing writer on aquatic insects, and fishes.

Peter is a professor of Biology at Jefferson Community College in Watertown, N.Y. He received a Bachelor of Science in Biology from St. Lawrence University and a Masters in Biology and Ecology from SUNY Potsdam. He has 36 years of experience teaching biology and ecology at high school and college levels. He received the SUNY Chancellors Award for Excellence in Teaching in 1993.

His articles have appeared in *The Conservationist* magazine. He has authored and co-authored several articles on the eastern coyote.

Peter is well known for his knowledge of the aquatic ecology of Tug Hill streams. He helped to develop a research based undergraduate course on determining water quality by focusing on macro-invertebrates.

Glenn Johnson - Contributing writer on reptiles, amphibians, molluscs, insects, other invertebrates, and birds.

Glenn is an authority on amphibians, reptiles, and invertebrates of Tug Hill. He received a Ph.D. from the SUNY College of Environmental Science and Forestry (SUNY ESF) in 1995, majoring in Conservation Biology, a Masters degree from SUNY ESF in 1989, majoring in Wildlife Ecology, and a Bachelors degree from SUNY Albany in 1976, majoring in Biology.

Glenn has been a visiting instructor at the SUNY ESF, Cornell University, SUNY Oswego, Colgate University, Onondaga Community College, and Wells College. He is currently teaching in the Biology Department at SUNY Potsdam.

He has published over a dozen papers and technical reports on mammals and reptiles. His articles have appeared in *The Conservationist* magazine.

Glenn has studied and inventoried frogs, turtles, and snakes for the NYS Herp Atlas in most of the quadrants on Tug Hill. He has led hundreds of field trips and seminars on frogs, snakes, and salamanders throughout Upstate New York.

Donald E. Moore III - Contributing writer on mammals.

Don is a wildlife biologist specializing in mammals. Don received a Bachelor of Science degree in Zoology (minor in entomology) from the SUNY College of Environmental Science and Forestry. He received a MPA in Economic Development from the Maxwell School of Syracuse University in 1990, and he is currently completing work on a doctorate at the SUNY College of Environmental Science and Forestry.

Don has been a visiting instructor at SUNY ESF, SUNY Oswego, SUNY Canton, and Onondaga and LaGuardia Colleges.

Don was Curator of Mammals at the Burnet Park Zoo in Syracuse from 1980-1993, after which he was the Director of the Thompson Park Zoo in Watertown from 1993-1995. While at Watertown Don directed the development of a zoo that features regional wildlife. Don is currently an Animal Curator with the Wildlife Conservation Society, New York.

He is an expert in mammals of the Tug Hill and Adirondack Regions. He has published over 36 articles on animal management, conservation education, and biodiversity conservation. He has had articles published in *Journey* magazine and *Highlights* magazine for children. He has worked as a technical advisor for the NYS Lynx Reintroduction Project and the World Conservation Union.

Lisa St. Hilaire - Contributing writer on herbaceous plants, ferns, mosses, and grasses.

Lisa received a Bachelor of Science in Environmental and Forest Biology, and a Master of Science in Plant Ecology from the SUNY College of Environmental Science and Forestry.

Lisa has a strong background in field experiences on the Hill studying plants and plant communities for The Nature Conservancy and the New York Natural Heritage Program. She surveyed historic locations of rare plants and natural communities on Tug Hill. Her ecological experiences include work as a wetland ecologist, community ecologist, and research assistant in the private and public sectors. She has teaching experience at high school and college levels.

Lisa has authored technical papers and presentations on plant ecology and plant community characteristics.

NOTES

NOTES

NOTES

NOTES